COLUMBIA HOME FRONT WARBOOKS

NUMBER 7

BOMBS, BUILDINGS AND SHELTERS
ARP for the Home

By WILLIAM H. HAYES

ASSISTANT PROFESSOR OF ARCHITECTURE

COLUMBIA UNIVERSITY

NEW YORK: MORNINGSIDE HEIGHTS

COLUMBIA UNIVERSITY PRESS

1942

COPYRIGHT 1942

COLUMBIA UNIVERSITY PRESS, NEW YORK

FOREIGN AGENTS: Oxford University Press, Humphrey
Milford, Amen House, London, E. C. 4, England, and
B. I. Building, Nicol Road, Bombay, India

MANUFACTURED IN THE UNITED STATES OF AMERICA

CONTENTS

I.	INTRODUCTION	1
II.	PERSONAL RISK AND TYPES OF BOMBS . . .	3
III.	CONSTRUCTION AND AIR-RAID PROTECTION .	29
IV.	SHELTERS	50
V.	MATERIALS AND CONSTRUCTION	76
	BIBLIOGRAPHY	82

PREFACE

THIS BOOKLET is based on a series of lectures, given at the request of the Columbia University Civilian Defense Council, which dealt with some aspects of civil air-raid protection of interest to the householder. General interest in the subject, as well as the nature of the discussions which followed the lectures, indicated the desirability of presenting in nontechnical terms, in so far as that is possible such parts of the great quantity of available technical data as are pertinent to the subject of domestic air-raid shelters.

In a booklet of this size, it is obviously impossible to treat exhaustively or even adequately all aspects of the subject. The present purpose is rather to foster interest, to present suggestions which may stimulate further study, and to provide for the layman a basic understanding of the fundamentals of the subject. The effects of bomb explosions on residential buildings are determined largely by the nature of the construction of these buildings. For this reason, a brief analysis of residential construction in terms of air-raid protection is included.

Credit is due Mr. Pokorny for his able assistance in assembling much of the data and for the colored illustrations which were used at the lectures and from which the figures in this report were made. To Professor William D. Turner, Professor William J. Krefeld, and Dr. E. C. Ingalls of Columbia University and Mr. Harry M. Prince, Architect of New York City, the author is indebted for advice and counsel.

WILLIAM H. HAYES

Columbia University
August, 1942

I. INTRODUCTION

PRIMARILY, active defensive as well as offensive efforts are a responsibility of the military forces. However, in total war, when the civilian is at war just as much as are the military, it is essential to have an alert and efficient civilian force organized for passive defense. The planning of adequate civil air-raid protection is one function of the civilian forces.

It is impossible to provide adequate air-raid protection on short notice. Therefore, it is the immediate responsibility of the civilian forces to study and to become familiar with the many complex economic and physical factors involved in the problem so that rational plans may be formulated for adequate protection.

The obvious purpose of civil air-raid protection measures is to provide physical protection for the civilian or home front force which in total warfare includes all persons in the community. Air-raid protection, however, performs also the less obvious although highly important function of helping to maintain the morale of the home front force. When thoughtful consideration is given to the problem of air-raid protection, it becomes increasingly evident that "Home safety is front line defense" in that it helps maintain the "Army behind the army."

The enlarging radius and severity of aerial warfare made possible by the ever-increasing range and efficiency of the airplane has extended danger zones to every person. Consequently, air-raid protection is a

INTRODUCTION

problem with which every householder is concerned. The largest part of our population is housed in small dwellings and small apartment buildings. Therefore, when the number of persons for whom shelters may be required is considered, the domestic shelter problem becomes by far the most important. The following chapters are concerned with this problem and its various solutions.

II. PERSONAL RISK AND TYPES OF BOMB

THE CIVILIAN, learning the extent of the destruction which bombs cause, wonders if these instruments of destruction are not endowed with some mysterious and awful supernatural power. The results of bombing, fantastic as well as awful, lend credence to such speculation. But despite the fact that aerial attack is for the civilian the most terrifying and destructive form of modern warfare, the probability of personal harm is small, if reasonable precautions are taken, because direct hits on buildings are proportional to the ratio of buildings to open space in the area under attack.

The total area vulnerable to attack, however, may be larger than the space occupied by the objects singled out for attack, despite the ability of the bombardier, under favorable conditions, to plant his bombs within a circle twenty-five or fifty feet in diameter. Many times bombs are distributed over so wide an area as to suggest indiscriminate bombing. Several factors contribute to wide distribution: the variation in the speed of the bombing plane, strong winds, low visibility, high altitude of the plane, and the hurried action of the bombardier because of antiaircraft fire. Consequently, it is possible that the objective or military target, though relatively small, may make a considerable adjacent nonmilitary area vulnerable to attack.

Safety from personal harm will vary according to the nature of the shelter which a person occupies during an attack. Where, then, should one seek shelter during an

RISK AND BOMB TYPES

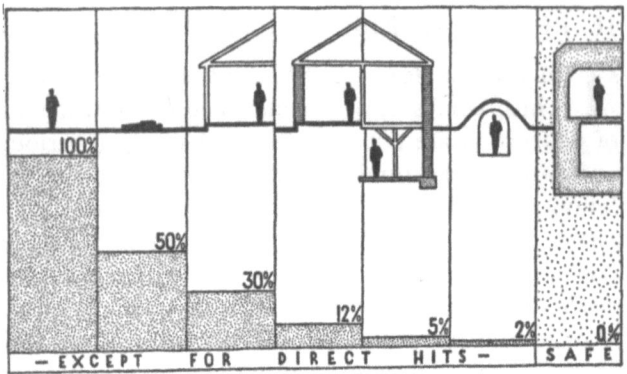

1. Degrees of Risk

Assuming a person standing unprotected in the open to be 100% vulnerable, experience indicates that the risk varies as follows: lying in the open, one-half; in a frame house, about one-third; in a solid masonry house, about one-eighth; in a reinforced basement, one-twentieth; and in an adequate outdoor shelter one-fiftieth as great.

air raid? Different places provide varying degrees of safety. Data from tests and actual experience give reasonably accurate facts. Some of these facts, compiled from information contained in a British air-raid handbook, are represented on Figure 1, which is "an approximate indication of the difference in the degree of risk resulting from taking cover in various ways."[1] On the lower part of the drawing is shown the relative percentage of risk to which one is exposed, assuming 100 percent vul-

[1] Ministry of Home Security, *Air Raids; What You Must Know, What You Must Do*, H. M. Stationery Office, London; *Architectural Forum*, January, 1942; New York *World-Telegram*, January 3, 1942.

RISK AND BOMB TYPES

nerability for a person standing in the open. The upper part of the drawing illustrates several ways of taking shelter. Reading from the left and showing increasing degrees of safety, they are: standing in the open, lying in the open (in the light of recent information, some authorities believe that merely lying down will not afford as much protection as is indicated because of the fragmentation hazard), and occupying a wood frame house, a house with solid brick walls, a reinforced basement, and an outdoor subsurface shelter such as an Anderson shelter. It must be pointed out that these data do not take into consideration direct hits, except in the case illustrated at the extreme right of the drawing where a "bombproof" is diagramed. The destructive power of most high-explosive bombs is so great that it is completely beyond the means of the individual to provide himself with a bombproof — that is, with complete protection. Consequently, it must be taken as an axiom that it is not feasible to attempt to build air-raid shelters for the home to withstand the direct hits of high-explosive bombs.

Figure 2 illustrates that a person's degree of risk, in an area under attack, may be greatly reduced if a shelter of some sort can be provided. Figure 2, A, shows an area subjected to attack. The person standing unprotected in this area is exposed to 100 percent risk because of the blast and splinters from bombs falling anywhere in the unshaded area. The size of the unshaded area is determined by the range of the blast and splinters of the bombs used; that is, the larger the bombs, and there-

RISK AND BOMB TYPES

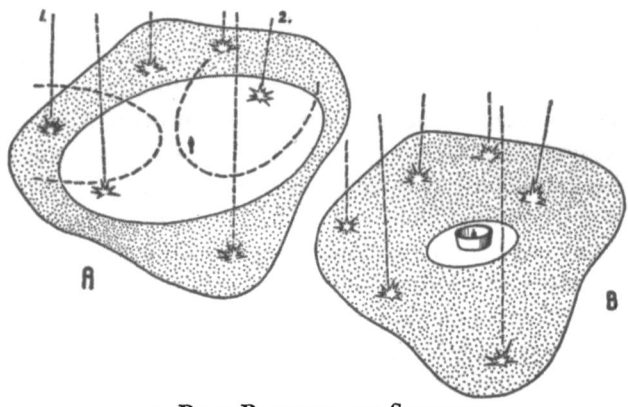

2. Risk Reduced by Shelters

An unprotected person is vulnerable to effects of bombs, of any given type, falling within unshaded area A. If a shelter is provided the risk under like conditions is reduced, and one is vulnerable only to effects of bombs falling within unshaded area B; the size of the latter depends on the adequacy of the shelter provided.

fore the greater their range of destruction, the greater the size of the unshaded area. The range of destruction of Bombs 1 and 2 is shown by the circular dotted lines. In Figure 2, B, it is assumed that the conditions are the same, except that a shelter or screen provides protection for the person. It is evident at a glance that the unshaded or danger area is greatly reduced. A small unshaded area exists because the shelter provided is not completely bombproof. The unshaded area would, for example, extend 50 feet beyond a 12-inch brick wall if the attack was made with 500-pound bombs, because such a wall will provide protection beyond this radius under such conditions.

RISK AND BOMB TYPES

Bombs

The civilian is concerned not so much with the technical details and ballistics of bombs as with the effects produced, because he is mainly interested in planning defenses to minimize the effects of these weapons. To do this efficiently, however, it is necessary to understand in a general way how they function and behave when detonated.

Low and high explosives:—The amount and kind of the explosive material contained in a bomb, together with the type of case or body, determine its behavior when detonated. "In general, an explosive is a substance (usually a solid) which, when subjected to heat and/or shock, is converted almost instantly into a very much larger volume of gas at a very high temperature and pressure.... Explosives are classed as low or high, according to the speed at which the conversion from a solid to a gas takes place."[2] A low explosive is changed from a solid to a gas by a process of rapid combustion. The conversion takes place at a less rapid rate than in the case of a high explosive. A high explosive is changed from a solid to a gas by a process of decomposition in an exceedingly rapid manner known as detonation. "The time required for the detonation of a 500-pound bomb is of the order of 1/10,000 of a second."[3] The potential

[2]Lt. Col. A. M. Prentiss, *Civil Air Defense,* New York: McGraw-Hill, 1941, p. 26.

[3]*Ibid.*

RISK AND BOMB TYPES

volume of gas generated and liberated from one cubic foot of an average high-explosive bomb (at the temperature associated with explosion) may be 10,000 to 12,000 cubic feet. Thus it is apparent that the atmosphere (or the earth itself) in contact with the rapidly expanding gas is suddenly and violently compressed by a blast or shock wave which moves rapidly outward in all directions from the point of origin, tending to shatter whatever happens to be within its zone of action. A low explosive, while acting in an exceedingly rapid manner, functions relatively more slowly and has a tendency to move or push, to displace air or earth without necessarily shattering it. "The destructive effect of an explosive is due, not so much to its potential energy, as to the extremely rapid rate at which that energy is developed. Thus, the characteristic effect of a low explosive is that of a push, whereas a high explosive shatters."[4] Present-day bombs therefore are made with the highly destructive high explosive materials. The three principal types used today are fragmentation bombs, general-purpose bombs, and demolition bombs.

Fragmentation bombs:—The fragmentation bomb is a small missile, weighing from 15 to perhaps 30 pounds; it is much used for attack on personnel in the field. The cylindrical casing or body of the bomb is encircled with scores or grooves that weaken the casing; this "ring" construction facilitates fragmentation of the relatively light casing into pieces of an effective size. Because the

[4]*Ibid.*

RISK AND BOMB TYPES

percentage of explosive is low and the casing light, these bombs do not have great blasting or penetrating power. Figure 3, B, shows a general view of a fragmentation bomb.

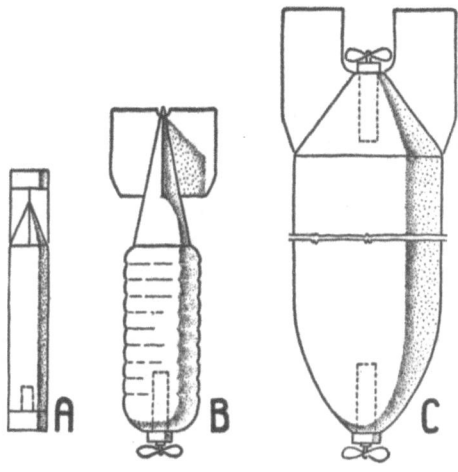

3. BOMB TYPES

Many kinds of bombs are used today, most of which are however variations of the three general types shown. The kilo-incendiary (A) is either cylinderical or hexagonal in form, about 2 inches in diameter and 14 inches long overall. The body of the kilo-incendiary is about 10 inches long. The fragmentation bomb (B) is about 4 inches in diameter, the body is approximately 12 inches long. These bombs vary in size. Demolition bombs (C) vary greatly in size, the heavy bombs may be 12 inches or more in diameter with a body length of 6 feet or more. Locations of fuse mechanisms are shown by dotted lines. Larger bombs are equipped with nose and tail fuses to increase likehood of detonation.

General-purpose bombs:—General-purpose bombs are made in weights of approximately 45 to 550 pounds and

RISK AND BOMB TYPES

may be equipped either with a delayed-action fuse (adjusted to explode the bomb after a predetermined time interval), which permits of some penetration of the target by the bomb before the explosion takes place, or with an instantaneous fuse, which causes the bomb to explode immediately on contact with an object. When equipped with delayed-action fuses, these bombs "will penetrate the upper floors of ordinary buildings and explode, causing considerable damage inside, or may demolish unprotected buildings by their blast effect if they explode close to the building on the ground outside."[5] Since these bombs are designed to produce effect mainly by blast, they are ineffective against specially protected or massive structures and deep targets. Because it is possible to carry a number of light-weight (100-to-250-pound) general-purpose bombs in a plane, and as this type of bomb is effective against the usual target, these bombs are generally used on bombing expeditions unless specific targets of great strength are the objectives, in which case demolition or "block-buster" bombs of great weight are used.

Demolition bombs:—Demolition bombs, generally used against special targets of military importance, vary in weight from 100 to 4,000 pounds. The smallest measure about 3 feet in length, the largest approximately 14 feet. The explosive charge comprises from as little as 25 percent to as much as 60 percent of the total weight, depending in part on whether the bomb has light, me-

[5]*Ibid.*, p. 25.

RISK AND BOMB TYPES

dium, or heavy case. The case is made thick or thin according to the job for which it is intended: a light-case bomb is designed to accomplish its purpose mainly by its blasting power, a heavy-case bomb by its penetrating and blasting power. Armor-piercing bombs are demolition bombs with cases heavy and tough enough to insure maximum penetration before explosion, a delayed-action fuse controlling the time of explosion. Aerial mines are demolition bombs with light cases arranged to explode on contact and are used chiefly against highly resistant targets. The larger bombs are difficult to transport, and their use is restricted to important targets of considerable size and strength, such as transportation lines, water supplies, industrial plants, warehouses, and the like. Figure 3 shows a general view of one of these bombs.

Sequence of events in a bomb explosion:—If events attendant on a bomb explosion are analyzed, the behavior and reactions of buildings subjected to attack can better be explained. Actually, events transpire so rapidly that it is difficult to appreciate the importance of everything which takes place. An analysis of a hypothetical case will perhaps illustrate best the different phases of a bomb explosion. If a 1,000-pound high-explosive bomb exploded on the surface of the ground some distance from where you were standing, you would observe the following events in the following order:

First, the flash of the explosion would be observed. (Light travels 186,000 miles per second.)

RISK AND BOMB TYPES

Second, the blast wave or wind motion in the atmosphere would be noted.

Third, the earth shock or vibration would be felt. Its violence would depend in part on the nature of the soil.

Fourth, the fragments would be heard landing near you, perhaps on roofs.

Fifth, the sound of the explosion would be heard. (Sound travels only approximately 1,100 feet per second.)

Your reaction would be to dodge or "duck" after it was all over.

It is apparent that the total destructive power of an explosion is the resultant of several factors which must be dealt with in any attempt to analyze its effects on structures. These factors are blast, fragmentation, and earth shock. Fire, which may break out as either a direct or an indirect result of an explosion, naturally is also a matter of concern.

Blast and fragmentation:—The blasting effect of a bomb explosion is produced by the sudden conversion of a relatively small volume of explosive charge (usually a solid) into a very much greater volume of gas. At normal temperatures this increase of volume may be 1,000 times. When the conversion takes place, a force is created so much greater than the force of normal atmospheric pressure that a pressure wave is sent out in every direction. A blast wave tends to expend its energy as rapidly as possible, and therefore pushes outward in every direction, from its point of

RISK AND BOMB TYPES

origin, faster than it can be absorbed by the atmosphere. It is much like a sound wave, except that its velocity and amplitude are much greater. Furthermore, a blast wave may be refracted, that is, diverted from its normal path of travel. It may also be reflected or "bounced off" a surface and turned back in a different direction. "Structures affected by blast are seldom isolated, but are usually grouped with others which interfere with the passage of the waves, causing reflection and refraction. In streets, when the blast is to some extent confined in a narrow space, the blast wave undergoes successive reflections"[6] and thus may be "bounced off" several different surfaces — walls, sidewalks, roofs, and so on. The waves, as they are refracted and reflected, and as they travel farther from their point of origin, change in frequency. That is, their frequencies vary at different distances from the bomb, and many times "sympathetic" or supplementary vibrations are induced in buildings at considerable distances. "As a result, windows at a distance may be broken, while those nearby subject to waves of different frequencies may remain undamaged."[7]

In the immediate vicinity of the explosion there is a violent disturbance of air for a radius of 10 to 30 feet, as shown on Figure 4 and 5 at A. The beginning of the blast wave is diagrammatically represented in these figures at B. The extent of this wave, whether 100 feet, 300

[6]*Protective Construction*, Structural Series Bulletin No. 1 (a Civilian Defense publication), Superintendent of Documents, Washington, D. C.
[7]*Ibid.*

RISK AND BOMB TYPES

feet, or more, depends largely on the size of the bomb.

The blast wave actually consists of two phases or components. The first is the "pressure phase" or initial pressure, mentioned above. This is followed by a less violent "suction phase." Even though the suction phase lasts longer than the pressure phase, both actions take place so rapidly as to be considered instantaneous, the total time consumed being about one thirtieth of a second. This sequence of action is significant. A building wall, for example, may be stable enough to withstand the first or pressure phase and remain in its normal position, even though the pressure phase is about five times greater than the suction phase, and yet may fail as a result of the subsequent suction phase. In such a case, the first phase may impair the strength of the wall so that the wall cannot withstand the suction force. This explains why the debris of bombed structures, pictures of which are seen in the press, is sometimes thrown or pushed into the building area and sometimes pulled or sucked into the adjoining yard or street.

"It has been observed that at distances close to the explosion pressure failures are more likely to occur than suction failures, because of the high intensity of the pressure phase, but at greater distances suction failures are more numerous than pressure failures. In general, if a structural element is equally resistant to pressure and suction effects, it will more likely fail in suction, since it may be greatly weakened by the preceding pressure."[8]

[8]Reprinted by permission from *Aerial Bombardment Protection* by H. E. Wessman and W. A. Rose, published by John Wiley & Sons, Inc., 1942.

RISK AND BOMB TYPES

Half of the blasting force may be spent in breaking the case of the bomb and accelerating — starting — the fragments on their flight. Nevertheless, the remaining strength of the bomb is many times (perhaps fifteen times) greater even than the impact energy discussed on page 39.

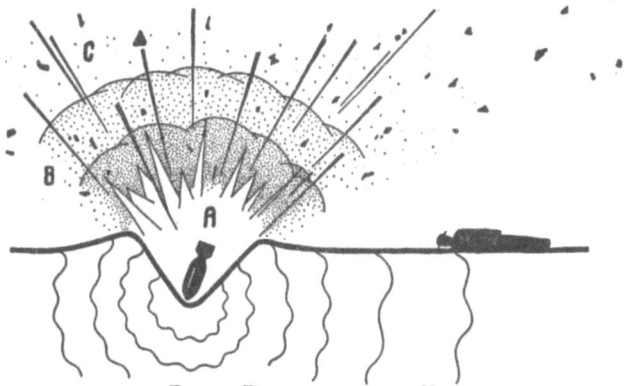

4. BOMB DETONATING IN EARTH

Fragmentation and, to a lesser degree, blast effects of a bomb exploded in relatively soft material may not spread out as far horizontally as when exploded on a relatively hard material (Fuse timing is also a factor.) Here the explosion occurs when the bomb has penetrated the earth before detonating. The angle of the cone-shaped volume in which the fragments are dispersed, is less than that shown in Fig. 5. Note also earth-shock waves proceeding outward from point of explosion.

Its explosion shatters most of the body or casing of the bomb into many small fragments. This process is known as fragmentation. Case fragments of irregular shape and various size fly in a radial pattern with starting speeds in some cases much greater than that of an

RISK AND BOMB TYPES

ordinary rifle bullet; however, this speed decreases rapidly. Figures 4 and 5, C, represent fragments being thrown from the center of the explosion. The force of these fragments is at times great enough to cause them to pierce brick and concrete walls. However, size and shape do not permit their maintenance of great speed and they may not fly great distances. Fragments from aerial gunfire are of little importance in comparison with the danger of fragments from bombs exploding on or near the ground, although aerial fragments may gain sufficient energy to injure unprotected personnel and roofs of light construction. Usually, the blasting effect of a bomb is, within a limited area, far greater than

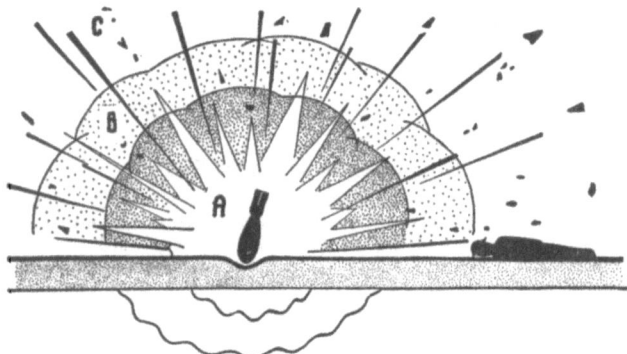

5. BOMB DETONATING ON HARD SURFACE

The area over which blast and fragmentation effects are spread in this case may be much greater than shown in Fig. 4; in fact, the danger volume may be said to be a hemisphere. The gaseous area of the explosion is shown, on both Figs. 4 and 5, at A; the start of the blast is diagramed at B, and fragmentation at C, which consists of fragments and splinters from the shell and other material caught in the path of the explosion.

RISK AND BOMB TYPES

its fragmentation effect and therefore is more important when general destructive results are considered.

The extent of the penetration of fragments into a material is dependent on their momentum and the area of the fragments in contact with the material. "In general, the greater the size and velocity of the fragment and the smaller the area in contact with the target, the deeper the penetration."[9]

The nature of the material on or in which a bomb explodes will alter the effect of the explosion. When a bomb penetrates a distance below the surface of a yard or lawn and then explodes as shown in Drawing 4, the blast wave and fragments are projected upwards throughout a cone-shaped area limited roughly in size by the excavation or crater made by the explosion. The angle of this cone may be considerably less than 180 degrees, and consequently areas relatively close to the explosion will be comparatively free from high-velocity fragments, as shown. The blast, however, will invade this area. If, on the other hand, a bomb is exploded on the surface, as for example on a pavement (as shown in Figure 5), the effective horizontal range of both blast and fragments is much greater — in fact, a full 180 degrees. Therefore, it is advisable to avoid exposure, in an air raid, on paved or other hard-surfaced areas, as the danger from fragments at least is somewhat greater in such a location.

Over how large an area are bombs destructive? From several sources data have been made available as to the

[9]Lt. Col. A. M. Prentiss, *Civil Air Defense*.

RISK AND BOMB TYPES

area of the danger zone. Naturally, these areas vary with the different bombs. It has been observed, in so far as blast is concerned, that the danger zone of a 100-pound bomb is in the vicinity of 100 feet in radius; of a 200-pound bomb, about 200 feet; of a 600-pound bomb, about 300 feet. These figures are approximate only, of course, because of the many variable circumstances which condition each instance and many times produce unbelievable results. The range of fragments from the above-mentioned bombs extends about 200 feet, 300 feet, and 400 feet. Fortunately, the strength or force of the blast and fragments decreases very rapidly with distance. "Everything in the immediate neighborhood of a big bomb therefore will be exposed suddenly to a violent pressure wave (blast) of many times atmospheric pressure, whereas, depending on the bomb, everything 50 feet away may be exposed only to two or three times atmospheric pressure. At 100 feet, the excess pressure (blast) may be only a fraction of an atmosphere."[10]

Facts concerning the extent of blast and fragmentation from the above-mentioned bombs are shown on Figure 6, where the weights of the bombs are given at the left and the distances in feet are shown along the lower edge. It will be seen that six 100-pound bombs will "cover" more area than one 600-pound bomb. That is to say that for general purposes the lighter bombs are more efficient than the heavier bombs. It has been pointed out that the ever-increasing effectiveness and capacities of bombing planes and the improvement of

[10]*Protective Construction*, Structural Series Bulletin No. 1.

RISK AND BOMB TYPES

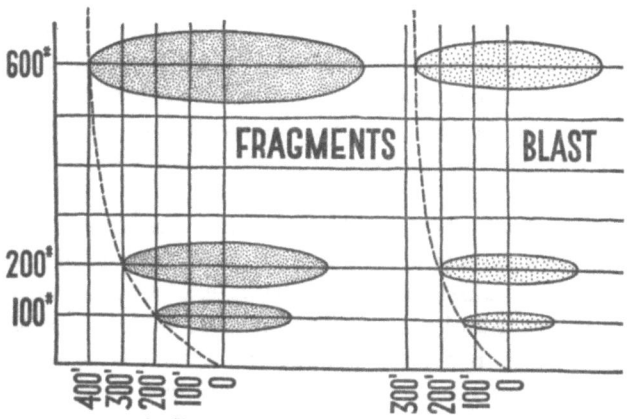

6. BLAST AND FRAGMENTATION

The relative sizes of areas of blast and fragmentation for three sizes of demolition bombs are shown. Weights of bombs are given at the left and the radii of the blast and fragmentation are as at the bottom. The danger from both blast and fragmentation decreases rapidly with distance; therefore danger at the outer limits of the blast and fragmentation areas may be small.

bomb sights and other equipment make bombing from great heights more feasible and that therefore heavier bombs may find greater use in the future. Even though the maximum velocity (the factor which determines to a great degree the kinetic energy or potential destructive power) of a bomb released from a plane can not be increased by merely dropping the bomb from a greater height (because beyond certain heights the velocity will not increase, since the resistance of the air will neutralize gravitational attraction), nevertheless the potential destructive power may be increased somewhat by increasing the mass or weight. In other words, because it

RISK AND BOMB TYPES

is becoming possible to dispatch bombs more accurately from heights so great that velocity no longer will increase the kinetic energy, it may become feasible to capitalize on the less important factor of mass or weight to increase the inherent destructive power of bombs.

Earth shock:—When a bomb strikes, penetrates, and then detonates in the earth, *earth shock* is produced: the explosion causes the earth to vibrate. Few phenomena are more troublesome at times or more baffling than vibration. It is a force that has long been recognized, though not generally too well understood. The vibrational effect, or earth shock, produced by a bomb explosion below the surface of the earth is similar to that of a local earthquake, except that earthquake movement may be said to be slower.

What is the nature of this shock or vibration? What factors are involved? When is it dangerous? The severity of a vibrational action (earth shock is a vibrational action or disturbance in the earth) is measured by: its *acceleration,* that is, an increase or decrease in its velocity; its *amplitude,* that is, its size; and its *frequency,* that is, number of vibrations per second. These factors are large or small depending mainly on the magnitude of the explosive charge and the nature of the ground— clay, loam, or rock, for example — in which the explosion occurs. Buildings on unstable ground are generally more severely damaged than those on firmer ground. Moist ground usually responds to earth shock more violently than does dry ground.

RISK AND BOMB TYPES

Another factor enters into consideration when the effect of earth shock on buildings is discussed: the frequency of vibration of the building itself. This factor involves discussion beyond the scope of this booklet; in passing, however, it should be noted that every building has a certain frequency of vibration, and if a similar vibration is set up outside the building and perhaps adjacent to it—in the earth, for example—the building may be caused to vibrate "sympathetically." While this obviously is not the controlling factor, it nevertheless may contribute to failure of the structure. More often the velocity and amplitude of the earth shock are great enough to cause destruction without any sympathetic vibration.

An example will, perhaps, illustrate how the earth reacts when disturbed by an explosion. When a stone is dropped into a still body of water, the resulting concentric ripples or waves travel outward, away from the point where the stone hit the water, with a decreasing velocity or deceleration and with decreasing amplitude or height. The frequency of the waves, that is, the number of waves that pass a given point in a certain space of time, depends in part on the impact with which the stone struck the water. This process is similar to what happens when a bomb explodes in the ground; waves or vibrations are generated. However, earth-shock waves are much more violent; they are, in fact, often violent enough to break rigid, inelastic, or nonflexible parts of buildings. Foundations built of masonry, which is an inelastic material, are in intimate contact

RISK AND BOMB TYPES

with the earth, and consequently are frequently broken by earth shock.

One other aspect of earth shock should be noted. Tests have recently disclosed the fact that earth shock operates through two components or phases, a vertical component which travels rapidly through the earth and a horizontal component which travels more slowly. Consequently, any subsurface structure, such as a foundation or a shelter, may be first lifted by the vertical component and then moved horizontally by the horizontal component. The effect on a nonflexible structure is obvious. Wall-bearing buildings and other unreinforced masonry buildings fare badly from the effects of earth shock.

Incendiary bombs:—Fire, both the friend and foe of man in peacetime, is an important implement of warfare. The weapon which uses fire as an agent of destruction is the incendiary bomb. The terrible destruction of life and materials when, even in peacetime, fires are inadvertently started emphasizes the great importance of preventing this destruction in wartime when many fires are deliberately and simultaneously started by the enemy through his use of incendiary bombs. It is commonly known that fire has caused a considerable percentage of the total destruction of European cities which have been subjected to aerial bombardment.

A constant and ever-present cause of fire waste is an inherent lack of resistiveness in residential construction. It is true that some communities (too few, how-

RISK AND BOMB TYPES

ever) prohibit the use of such inflammable materials as wood shingles for roofing, and wood frame construction is not permitted in certain districts. Despite these precautions, other minor safeguards, and legal regulations, 18 percent of the annual fire loss is chargeable to the "exposure hazard" that is, to fire started outside the building. In other words, existing structures, particularly residential buildings, are exceedingly vulnerable to the spread of fire. Consequently, in densely settled areas and in cities, always focal points of attack, the hazard that separate fires, started by incendiaries and by high-explosive bombs, will merge into a conflagration is enormous. In fact, a prime objective in an incendiary attack is conflagration.

"The use of fire to dislodge an enemy from a position, to destroy his stores and his abode, goes back far in the history of the human race."[11] It is revealed that "the Assyrians were acquainted with liquid fire, probably petroleum from seepages of what are now the Iraq oil fields, and that they employed this in military operations. Flaming arrows and balls of burning pitch thrown from catapults were not unusual in antiquity and in the Middle Ages."[12] The Greeks used a material "said to have been a mixture of pitch, sulphur, quicklime, and naphtha. It was squirted from siphonlike devices and, once ignited, continued to burn even on water, adding a touch of the supernatural to the instinctive animal

[11] J. Enrique Zanetti, *Fire from the Air*, New York: Columbia University Press, 1942.
[12] *Ibid.*

RISK AND BOMB TYPES

fear of fire."[13] With the invention of modern implements of warfare, fire as a weapon was neglected until the development, in recent times, of the airplane. Aerial bombing has once again made fire an effective weapon.

Today the danger to civilians from aerial bombardment is large because no distinction is made between military targets and civilians by the bombs and because the ballistics of incendiary bombs are bad—these bombs cannot be aimed. The incendiary bomb is the greatest menace to the average home. It is an effective weapon, and therefore its continued use may be expected.

It should be understood that generally the incendiary bomb does not explode on impact or at any subsequent time, and therefore measures to extinguish it may be taken immediately. A small percentage of all incendiaries used have contained small amounts of explosives for the purpose of scattering the burning incendiary material (which forms the larger part of the bomb) over a greater radius, thus increasing the hazard of fire over a greater area. These small explosive charges are also intended to discourage efforts to put out the bomb. However, if one will keep calm and use reasonable care, he can easily and quickly extinguish these bombs. The fact that they are persistent in their action, prolonging their destructive work, makes it imperative promptly to combat such action.

The ordinary incendiary bomb (see Figure 3, A) is so made that when it strikes, the impact causes the fuse mechanism to set off a priming mixture, which is the

[13]*Ibid.*

RISK AND BOMB TYPES

material inside the bomb. The priming mixture in the magnesium-thermite bomb, composed of approximately one part by weight of metallic aluminum and three parts of iron oxide, is called "thermite." When the thermite is ignited, the heat of combustion (over 5,000 degrees F.) is great enough to ignite the magnesium alloy of which the casing or body of the bomb is made. When magnesium is alloyed with aluminum and copper it is known as electron; hence the term "electron bomb." The term "kilo bomb" or "kilo-incendiary," also used in connection with incendiaries, is applied to those bombs weighing one kilogram or 2.2 pounds. Incendiary bombs are made in weights ranging from 2.2 pounds to about 50 pounds. The smaller ones, 2 to 4 pounds, are more generally used. It will be observed from the above that all of the material used in constructing such bombs serves to start fires. It should also be noted that these bombs are light in weight, considering their size. Aluminum weighs about 170 pounds a cubic foot and magnesium only 112 pounds. Compared to steel, which weighs about 490 pounds a cubic foot, these are lightweight materials. Consequently, a relatively large number of these highly efficient bombs may be carried by one plane.

When an incendiary bomb is first ignited, the thermite burns fiercely within the bomb casing for a short period of time — less than a minute — before the magnesium casing itself is ignited. The burning of the casing produces an intense heat and a dazzling flame. No noise except a hissing sound is produced, which makes discov-

RISK AND BOMB TYPES

ery more difficult during an air raid when other things are producing considerable noise.

To combat the action of these bombs several methods may be used. A spray of water may be played on the bomb. The water spray will not extinguish the fire; it will, however, increase the rate of combustion (because additional oxygen is fed to the flame via the water), and consequently the time during which the bomb will burn will be decreased. This naturally reduces the danger of igniting adjacent inflammable materials. The flame will increase when the spray of water is applied. The spray will not, however, cause the burning to become so violent that burning particles of magnesium will be thrown off, possibly to lodge on inflammable materials near by. It is possible to combat an incendiary with a spray of water so that it will burn itself out in two or three minutes after the spray is applied. The fact should not be overlooked that any surface on which the burning bomb rests is subjected to terrific heat. If sand and a long-handled shovel or hoe are at hand, the bomb may be rolled, while burning, onto a sand bed laid to insulate the floor.

More recently, another method of attacking these bombs has been tried; in this, a jet of water is applied directly to the burning portion of the bomb. This procedure increases the rate and violence of burning to such a degree that burning particles of magnesium are thrown off. These particles quickly burn themselves out, however, and when there is an open or unoccupied space in the vicinity of the action they are not a serious

RISK AND BOMB TYPES

hazard. The force of the stream of water will generally cause the burning particles to fly away from the operator of the water jet; consequently, his risk is not materially increased by this method. Nevertheless, the operator should always provide himself with some sort of shield as a protection. The stream of water will not extinguish the bomb; rather, because of its force, it will tend to knock or break apart the burning part of the bomb, and if the stream of water is efficiently handled, this part will be completely and quickly disengaged from the remainder, so that a large portion of the bomb may not be entirely consumed by fire. It is possible to combat an incendiary with a jet of water so that its burning will cease in less than a minute after the jet is applied. At a recent demonstration, identical 4-pound incendiary bombs were extinguished: first, by a spray of water applied by experienced operators, from a stirrup pump in 65 seconds; second, by a jet of water applied by an experienced operator, from a stirrup pump in 15 seconds. Early instructions were to attack incendiaries with a spray. Later experience has definitely established the fact that the jet method is the more effective way to attack these bombs. The spray method is not abandoned; however, because of the time element the jet method is generally recommended.

That it is imperative to extinguish incendiary bombs as rapidly as possible is realized by one who has a relative idea of the heat developed by these bombs. If the magnesium alloy casing of a kilo bomb is ignited and not extinguished, it will burn for perhaps 8 or 10 min-

RISK AND BOMB TYPES

utes and will give off approximately 8,000 B.t.u. of heat. (The B.t.u. is the unit of measure of quantity of heat.) This is about the quantity of heat produced in the same time by the average hand-fired coal-burning boiler in the average-sized home. However, the intensity of the heat produced by the magnesium fire is much greater than that of the coal fire, and also the heat of the former is concentrated on a relatively small area.

Several materials other than water have been suggested for use in extinguishing incendiary bombs. Ordinary clean sand will be found effective. It must be dry and free from vegetable or other foreign matter. Washed sand such as is used for building purposes is satisfactory. Beach sand, if it is clean and dry, is also acceptable. The latent heat of fusion of salt is approximately 500 times greater than the specific heat of sand; in other words, salt will "consume" a large quantity of heat, and consequently "free-running" salt is effective in extinguishing incendiaries. Rock salt is not satisfactory because the lumps contain globules of moisture. A mixture of salt (about 95 percent) and tar or pitch, sold under various proprietary names, will be found effective. Dry sand may be conveniently stored in stout paper tubular containers; these, as well as similar containers in which the salt and tar mixtures are packaged, facilitate pouring the extinguishing material on the burning bomb. A layer of linoleum as a floor covering may prove valuable in that it will prevent burning magnesium, which is a liquid and which behaves much like mercury, from flowing into cracks in a wood floor.

III. CONSTRUCTION AND AIR-RAID PROTECTION

THE QUESTION which is uppermost in every householder's mind, in so far as aerial bombardment is concerned, is: Does the average house or apartment provide adequate air-raid protection? To answer this question, it is first necessary to evaluate, in terms of air-raid protection, the several common types of house construction. Such evaluation will show that some types of construction have great strength and resistance and others great weakness and inability to resist any considerable stress under bombardment.

It is not to be inferred that, because a particular type of construction is especially vulnerable to the effects of bombing, it is not entirely safe and stable under normal conditions. Rather, the inference is that aerial bombardment imposes unusual conditions on buildings normally designed to withstand these conditions. On the other hand, the fact should not be lost sight of that all buildings offer some resistance to demolition and therefore provide some degree of protection. The adequacy of protection depends upon the inherent stability of the building. This inherent stability may, after a careful survey, be found inadequate, in which case it may prove reasonable to reinforce the structure in various ways in order to increase its protection to the point of safety. On the other hand, it should be noted that British experience has shown clearly that some types of construction are possessed of a much greater reserve strength than usual structural design theory would lead one to suppose.

Any analysis of construction must deal with the normal stability incorporated in the structure, if an evaluation of its worth to resist attack is to be made.

Light Wood Frame Construction

It is commonly known that the most usual type of home construction in this country is "light wood frame construction." Approximately 90 percent of all homes are of wood frame construction. In its present form it is indigenous to this country. Frame houses abroad employ heavier members rigidly fastened together and differ in many other ways from our wood construction. The present-day American wood frame is an exceedingly light-weight assembly characterized by many small members easily handled, placed close together, and held in place by a few wire nails — sometimes too few. It developed in answer to a demand for a rapid and economical form of construction, and it must be said that it answers that demand reasonably well.

Figure 7 illustrates the basic structural parts of this construction, which may be described as a "cratelike" structure. It is similar to a crate in that it is very light in weight and rather fragile when subjected to abnormal stresses and strains. This is so because it has been "refined," from a structural design point of view, to such a degree that it may be built with a minimum amount of both material and labor.

CONSTRUCTION AND ARP

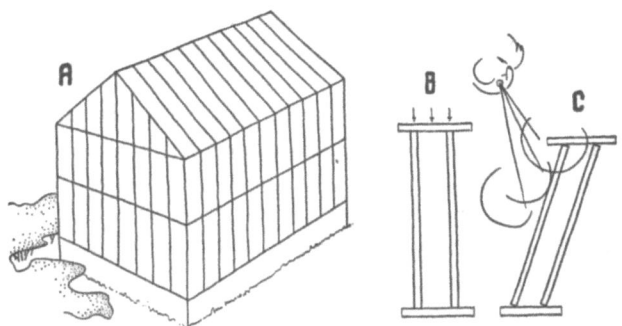

7. THE WOOD FRAMED HOUSE
A, basic structural parts of "cratelike" common light wood frame construction. B, any two of the sticks or "studs" which are the vertical structural members of the frame shown at A. These studs are strong enough to support usual vertical load, but are less strong to resist such lateral or sidewise loads as may be imposed by the blast from an explosion, as shown at C.

It will be observed, as shown by Figure 7, A, that many small vertical two-by-four-inch sticks called studs function not only as the principal members of the walls but also as supports for all floors above the first. These members are fixed at the top by a horizontal plate and at the intermediate floors by another horizontal band, and they rest upon a horizontal plate or sill placed on top of the foundation. This series of sticks, if maintained in a vertical position, loaded vertically, and arranged as shown in Figure 7, B will support a considerable weight. However, such a structure will not resist large lateral or sidewise forces such as are shown in Figure 7, C and such as are brought into play by the blast of a bomb. A horizontal sheathing or covering of one-inch boards, ap-

CONSTRUCTION AND ARP

plied to the outer face of the studs strengthens the whole assembly and makes it sufficiently stable under normal conditions.

Even greater stability is given such a construction if a brace is introduced (as shown in Figure 8, A) or if the covering is applied diagonally (as shown in Figure 8, B). Figure 8, C, shows braces and diagonal sheathing applied to the frame. Diagonal sheathing will increase rigidity from four to seven times.

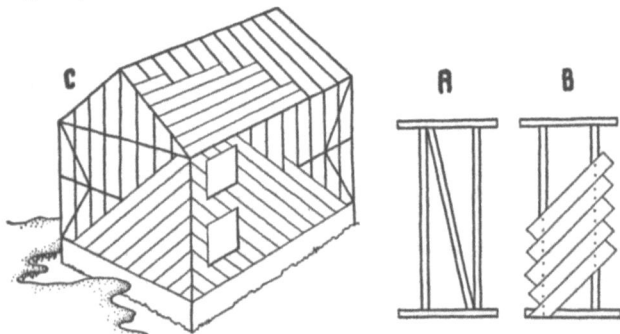

8. THE BRACED WOOD FRAME HOUSE

A, a method for increasing the stability of the house frame shown in Figure 7. The diagonal brace is often installed as shown, or bracing of the frame may be accomplished through the use of diagonal boards or "sheathing," as shown at B. C illustrates a frame in which both braces and diagonal sheathing are used. Present FHA specifications require facing of one sort or another.

The frame of the house is adequate to carry the usual weight placed on it — the furniture and occupants — and to resist such forces as that of wind. Wind pressure, however, is not great as compared to the blasting force of a bomb explosion. A 60-mile gale will create a pres-

CONSTRUCTION AND ARP

sure against a wall of approximately 12 pounds a square foot. Hurricanes which have demolished houses may at 120 miles per hour create pressures of 45 pounds a square foot. The blasting force of a 600-pound medium-case bomb exploding 25 feet away from a wall may under certain conditions create a pressure of 3,600 pounds a square foot on the wall. The frailness of the frame house in the face of such a terrific force is all too apparent.

There are no complete data on the behavior of our light wood frame construction when subjected to actual bombing. Tests simulating bombing conditions indicate that frame walls are only slightly resistant to blast and splinters from a 600-pound bomb exploded 50 feet away. Of all common forms of construction, a frame wall with a wood covering (shingles or siding) is probably the least resistant to blast and splinters.

Because frame construction is slightly elastic, is not completely rigid, it is possible that it may react to the less severe effects of blast rather better than is now expected.

Masonry Veneer

A large number of homes today are of brick veneer construction. This is not fundamentally another type of construction; rather, it is a variation of the wood frame — the wood frame "clothed" in brick. The term brick veneer merely designates the kind of finish placed over the outside walls of a wood frame building. This construction is shown diagrammatically on Figure 9, A. It will be noticed that the brickwork is only one brick

CONSTRUCTION AND ARP

or four inches in thickness and that its only function is that of a cover or exterior finish. It does not help to support the structure; in fact, the brick is secured at intervals to the wood frame by metal anchors as shown at Figure 8, B. In back of this brick covering (or stone, which is sometimes used in this manner) will be seen the identical wood frame illustrated on Figures 7 and 8.

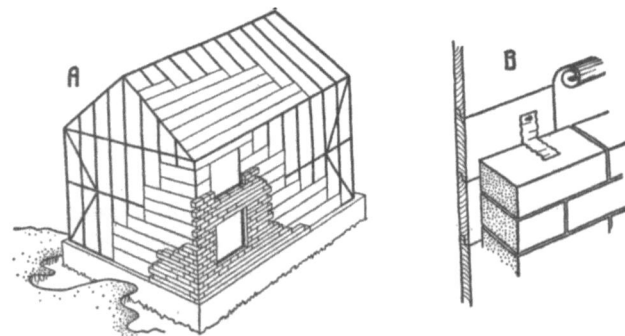

9. THE MASONRY VENEER HOUSE

A, the fundamental structural parts of the veneer (usually brick) house. It is essentially the same construction as that employed in the frame house. The brick veneering (B) serves merely as an exterior cover and does not support any weight. Being thicker (4 inches) and heavier than other cover materials, such as shingles or siding, the masonry cover provides greater resistance to splinter penetration.

This brick covering, being a substantial and durable material and being thicker and heavier than other coverings such as stucco, clapboard, or shingles of wood, asbestos, or composition, probably does afford a slightly greater protection from the effects of blast and, to a lesser degree, from splinter penetration than do the

CONSTRUCTION AND ARP

thinner exterior finishes. Again it must be noted that there is not a great deal of data available on the behavior of this type of wall under actual bombing conditions. But tests show that four-inch brick veneer is not completely resistant to splinter perforation from a 600-pound bomb detonated at a distance of 50 feet. Such a wall would be damaged severely by blast and splinters from a 300-pound bomb at 25 feet. But a masonry veneer wall is probably more resistant to blast and penetration than is a frame wall.

Masonry Wall-bearing Construction

Many private homes and row houses as well as small apartments and commercial buildings are erected with masonry (brick, stone, or concrete-block) exterior walls. In such a method of construction these are actually bearing walls, that is, they support the floors, roofs, partitions, and so on. The elements of such a construction are shown on Figure 10, A. This is a boxlike construction, the exterior masonry walls forming the sides of the box while the interior of the box is subdivided both horizontally by floors and roof and vertically by partitions built of the cratelike wood frame construction described above. The very nature of the masonry walls employed gives this form of construction more durability and greater stability than wood frame construction. The sheer weight of the masonry, the tenacity of the cementing material or mortar used to "glue" the masonry units together, and the bulk of these walls

CONSTRUCTION AND ARP

contribute to the safety and stability of this construction under usual conditions. These walls, if properly built, are entirely adequate to support the vertical loads placed on them by the floors and roofs. The three arrows, Figure 10, B, represent the normal vertical loads. But bomb explosions produce abnormal loads via blast. The three arrows, Figure 10, C, represent loads which may be produced by the blast of an explosion and which are not vertical but horizontal, sidewise, or la-

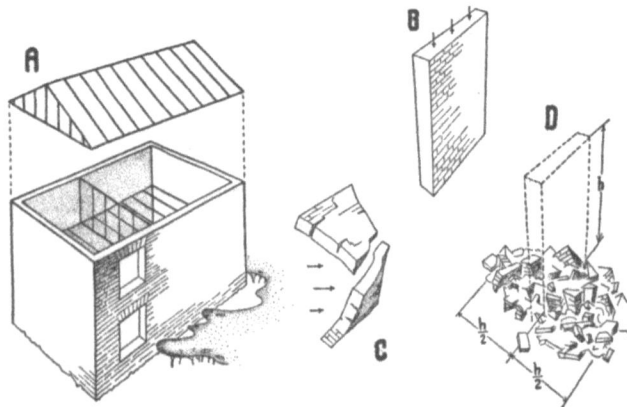

10. THE MASONRY OR WALL-BEARING HOUSE

The house built of masonry, stone, brick, etc., is a "boxlike" assembly (A). The interior and roof construction is of wood—the same construction that is used in the frame house. Like the wood framed wall, the masonry wall (B) is capable of supporting the usual vertical loads imposed upon it, but, also like the frame wall, it does not possess great lateral stability to resist unusual sidewise loads (C) and such as might be imposed by blast. The two phases of a blast—the pressure phase and the suction phase—often cause a masonry wall to collapse (D) that is, the debris of the wall may be deposited on both sides of the original location of the wall.

CONSTRUCTION AND ARP

teral. The resistance of masonry walls to these loads is not great, and failure may occur as shown.

Experience has proved that, because of the action of blast and suction resulting from bomb explosions, a wall of units of masonry is likely to collapse as illustrated at Figure 10, D, the remains of the wall being disturbed about equally on each side of the original position of the wall, which is indicated by the dotted lines. This fact establishes a rule or precept as to the location of outdoor shelters in relation to adjacent buildings: it is desirable to locate an outdoor air-raid shelter away from adjacent buildings a distance equal to at least one half the height of the outside walls of these adjacent buildings. It is obvious that such a location will appreciably reduce the hazard of building debris falling on the shelter. The weight of this material is considerable; a brick wall 8 inches thick, forming one side of a two-story house 25 feet long, weighs about 34,000 pounds or 17 tons. A wood frame wall of the same dimensions will weigh about 4 tons.

Floors

Purposely, to this point no analysis of floor structure has been made because the structural arrangement of all conventional nonfireproof wood floors is substantially the same in wood frame buildings and in buildings of wall-bearing construction. These horizontal surfaces, the floors, may be visualized as a series of superimposed shelves, supported in the wood frame building

CONSTRUCTION AND ARP

by the vertical sticks or studs which form the cratelike frame work and in the wall-bearing building by the boxlike arrangement of masonry walls.

Wood framed floors:—The essential parts of the wood framed floor are shown on Figure 11. The principal members, called beams or joists, support all other parts

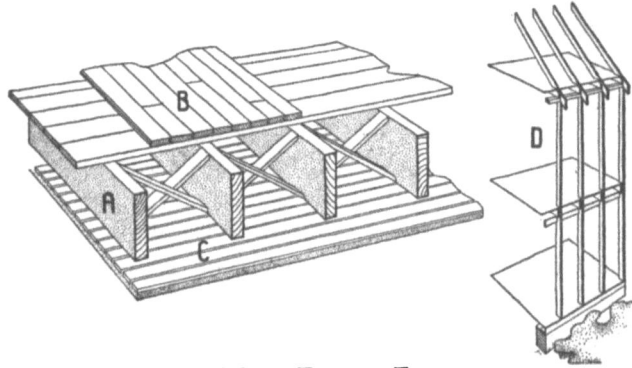

11. WOOD FRAMED FLOORS

The principle members of the floor assembly, the members that support the whole assembly, are those marked A, on top of which are placed two layers of floor boards (B). The ceiling of the room below (C) is hung from the bottom of the beams. Criss-cross bracing or "bridging" installed as shown increases greatly the stability of the whole assembly. The under layer of floor boards is frequently laid diagonally, this also increases stability. Each floor in a wood frame structure (D) is assembled in this manner.

of the assembly and whatever weight that may be placed on the two layers of flooring which rest on top of the beams. The material of the ceilings of the rooms below (if there are any), such as lath and plaster, is also sup-

CONSTRUCTION AND ARP

ported by these beams. Flat roofs are constructed in a like manner except that only one layer of boards is placed on top of the beams. On this board surface is laid a weatherproof roofing material of asphalt paper or sheet metal. Pitched roofs are similarly constructed, the chief difference being in the finished weatherproof roofing material, which is usually of wood, composition, tile, or slate shingles. Current practice is to use relatively thin pieces of material for beams and then reinforce or brace them laterally with crisscross bridging, as shown. This arrangement also helps, together with the floor boards above, to distribute any concentration of weight which might be imposed on the floor; thus, the whole assembly is entirely adequate to support the usual loads. However, a floor subjected to unusual loads such as are imposed by a falling bomb is able to offer relatively little resistance to the inherent kinetic energy of the bomb.

In order to gain an idea of the enormous amount of inherent energy possessed by a falling bomb, neglect for the moment the bomb's tendency to penetrate or pierce the surface with which it comes in contact and consider only its impact or striking power.

The magnitude of the impact energy or power of a falling bomb is increased if the bomb is dropped from a great height (up to certain limits) rather than from a low altitude. The weight of the bomb is also a factor: the heavier the bomb the greater its inherent power. The speed of the plane from which the bomb is released is still another, although lesser, factor; that is, the

CONSTRUCTION AND ARP

greater the "initial velocity" of the bomb the greater its inherent energy or power. Thus it will be observed that a 100-pound bomb released from a plane flying at an altitude of 10,000 feet and at a rate of 200 miles per hour will possess more inherent energy to do damage than will the same bomb dropped from 5,000 feet, from a plane traveling at the same rate. Again, if the speed of the plane is increased, the potential bomb energy will be increased. It is apparent that innumerable conditions of bomb release will produce innumerable effects. Actually, the bomb mentioned above, released at an altitude of 5,000 feet, if brought to rest by a construction will have imparted to that construction an impact load of over 500,000 pounds.

In residential buildings, floors are designed to support a superimposed weight of 40 pounds over every square foot of their surfaces; roofs are designed to support slightly less. This means, for example, that the usual wood beam 3 inches thick and of the required width, placed over a 17- or 18-foot room, is designed to support about 1,000 pounds. If it is assumed that three such beams act together in supporting a load because of the way in which the crisscross bridging functions, it then may be said, for our purpose, that the beams will actually support a uniform load of about 3,000 pounds. Obviously the collapse of any usual construction, be it roof, wall, or floor, is inevitable under the terrific impact of a falling bomb, even though the resiliency of the construction will absorb part of the energy of the bomb.

CONSTRUCTION AND ARP

The smaller incendiary bombs do not develop an impact or striking energy anything like the heavier bombs but are nevertheless capable of penetrating roofs of the usual type of wood construction.

Fireproof floors:—Habitational buildings over six stories in height are, in many communities, required by law to be of fireproof construction. This necessitates the use of masonry materials and of steel adequately protected from fire by masonry materials. The most common type of construction of this kind is illustrated on Figure 12, which shows use of a reinforced concrete

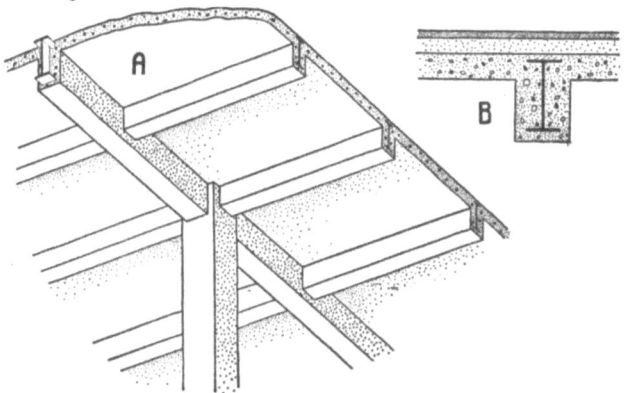

12. FIREPROOF FLOORS

A, a section of a fireproof floor construction as viewed from below. Horizontal steel beams running in two directions are supported by occasional vertical steel posts or columns. Concrete fireproofing completely encases all steel members. The spaces between the beams are filled by concrete slabs on which the finished flooring is laid. B, a sectional view of a floor beam, floor slab, and fireproofing.

slab at least 4 inches thick supported by steel floor beams encased in concrete as a protection from fire. The finished floor, whether of cement, linoleum, cork, or wood, is laid on top of the concrete slab. Fireproof roof construction is similar. This type of construction is much less vulnerable to the effects of bombs than is wood construction. The 4-inch floor or roof slab will generally stop the travel of an incendiary bomb. It can be readily pierced by the heavier bombs. Four or five such floors, however, do provide considerable overhead protection.

Various Types of Residential Building

Because of land values and other economic and social factors, residential buildings in different communities develop in different ways. That is, in certain districts, in addition to single-family dwellings, there are found attached or row houses, and in other districts apartment houses are erected. In many of the older districts of our cities will be found tenement houses and converted dwellings.

Private houses:—Generally, it will be found that one- and two-family houses are built of light wood frame or brick veneer of the types illustrated in Figure 7, 8, and 9.

Row houses:—The majority of attached or row houses built in urban areas are of wall-bearing construction, as are also most apartment houses (multiple dwellings)

CONSTRUCTION AND ARP

six stories and less in height. Figure 13 shows the basic parts of several nonfireproof wall-bearing row houses. It will be noted that these houses are built in substantially the same way as the individual wall-bearing house illustrated in Figure 10. The masonry bearing walls, which separate the individual units of a block of row houses, constitute effective barriers against the travel of fire from one unit to another; in fact, they are known as fire walls. These walls also minimize and tend to restrict the effects of blast and splinter action of bomb explosions. On the other hand, the resistance offered

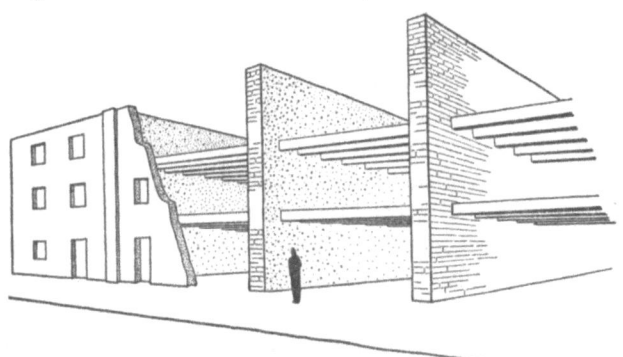

13. NON-FIRE PROOF ATTACHED OR ROW HOUSES

If the front wall, roofs and all non-structural materials were to be removed from a block of row houses, the basic structural members of the construction would be exposed to view and would appear much as shown. Each unit of a block of attached houses, whether of simple rectangular form with flat roofs or built with more complex forms and covered with pitched roofs, are generally separated by masonry "party walls" which normally act not only as supports for the floors but also as "fire walls" and tend to restrict the spread of fire at all times. The effects of blast and fragmentation are also somewhat reduced by these walls.

CONSTRUCTION AND ARP

by the several floors of row houses and nonfireproof apartments to bomb penetration unfortunately is not appreciable. A plan reasonably typical for row houses is shown on Figure 18.

Tenement houses:—The term tenement house generally is used to designate a multifamily structure built some years ago, during a period when concepts of housing and laws regulating the construction of dwellings were decidedly inadequate, judged by today's standards. Many thousands of these buildings, which are moral, social, and economic liabilities, still are tenanted by families whose economic condition does not permit of better housing. There are about 67,000 buildings of this category in New York City alone, ranging from four to seven stories in height. Figure 19, A, shows a more or less typical plan of these buildings, which have masonry (usually brick) exterior bearing walls. The interior construction is wholly of wood, including the stairs and halls. There is no reasonably safe shelter in any part of these buildings as they now exist. Obviously, these structures constitute a hazard and a liability to a community even in normal peacetime. In war, the potentialities of disaster of these buildings with their large population is terrible to contemplate, as it is probable that these areas will be given particular attention during an incendiary attack.

Converted buildings:—With the passing of years, some residential districts, originally areas of single-family

CONSTRUCTION AND ARP

city houses, change in such a way as to become suitable locations for multifamily buildings. This has occasioned the remodeling of many of these single-family dwellings into apartment houses or rooming houses called converted dwellings. A typical plan of one of these converted dwellings is shown on Figure 19, B. The construction of these buildings is identical with that of the tenement house described above, and therefore it is apparent that they offer no more air-raid protection. Fortunately, converted buildings are not usually as large and populous as the tenement houses and therefore the destruction of a converted building would involve less loss of life.

"New law" nonfireproof apartments:—The more recently built nonfireproof apartment houses have public halls and stair halls of fireproof construction. Figure 20 illustrates a "new law" nonfireproof apartment building six stories high. On this drawing the fireproof hall and stair enclosure, from the street entrance to the roof, appears as a "core" in the central part of the building. It is virtually just that—a substantial construction of fireproof materials. The surrounding interior construction, however, is wood frame. This core affords the best shelter in such a building.

Fireproof apartments:—One type of construction fundamentally different from the above types is used occasionally in the erection of residential buildings. It is fireproof, considerably more expensive than the non-

CONSTRUCTION AND ARP

fireproof constructions, and employed mostly for large apartment buildings. Its construction involves a "skeleton" of structural steel or of reinforced concrete. In either case, the skeleton is the structural element of

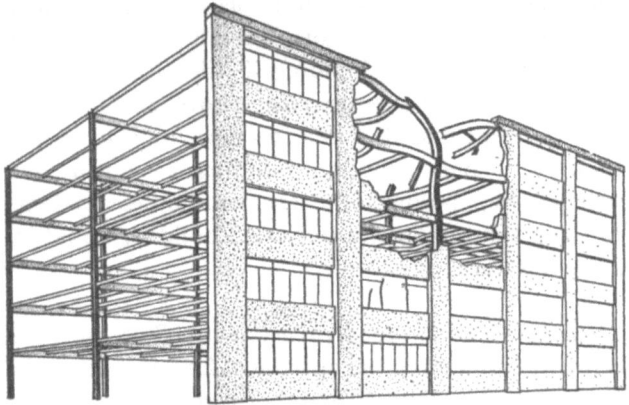

14. SKELETON BUILDINGS

In this system of construction, whether of steel or reinforced concrete, the "skeleton" is the structural or load-carrying part of the building. It is fireproof. At the left the non-structural parts, walls, floor panels, roof, and etc., are shown removed, thus exposing the structural skeleton or frame of steel. The nature of this construction—substantial, tough and somewhat elastic—is such that the effects of bombing are often local. That is, damage is often confined, as shown here, to the immediate vicinity of the explosion. The fire hazard is also small. The interior spaces on the intermediate floors of these buildings afford the best protection to be found in any of our usual types of buildings.

the building, and all other parts, such as floor and roof panels, walls, and so on, are supported on the steel skeleton or on a reinforced concrete skeleton. Figure 14 diagrammatically illustrates a steel-skeleton building;

CONSTRUCTION AND ARP

the reinforced concrete skeleton is similar. The floor and roof construction of these structures is generally that illustrated in Figure 12. Because of the great strength of the materials used and the manner in which the several structural members are fastened together, these structures offer great resistance to bombardment. In the steel skeleton the various parts are either riveted or welded together. In the reinforced concrete skeleton all structural parts are poured together and are virtually monolithic. Thus, great stability is given these constructions—so much, in fact, that bombardment damage is often local, that is, only the part of the building that is hit is severely damaged, as shown by the drawing.

Foundations

One other major element of structure must be considered to make the picture complete. One might think that the foundation of a building, being below the ground, would be immune to aerial bombardment. It is, of course, a fact that this part of a building is not as vulnerable, in so far as blast and splinters are concerned, as is the superstructure. However, bombs, for several reasons, often find their way into the earth before detonating. When a bomb penetrates the earth and there explodes, it not only excavates a considerable amount of the earth in its immediate vicinity but also causes the earth shock discussed above. This vibrational effect, similar to that of a local earthquake, produces unusual stresses on any near-by foundation.

CONSTRUCTION AND ARP

Most foundation walls, as built today of stone, poured concrete, or hollow concrete blocks, are strong enough under usual conditions. A wall built of hollow concrete blocks—a much-used material—as shown at A on Figure 15, will not resist the lateral (sidewise) force of earth shock as well as a monolithic wall made of

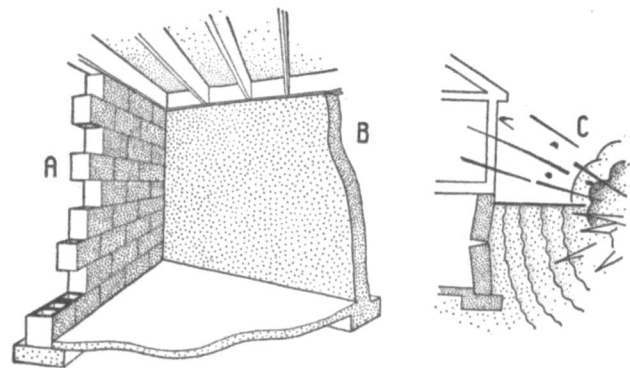

15. FOUNDATIONS

The majority of homes are placed on top of continuous masonry-bearing walls or foundations built (A), of units of masonry or (B) of monolithic concrete. Foundations are especially vulnerable to earth shock (C). Generally, monolithic walls and thick walls of stone if well built have greater lateral stability to resist earth shock than the thinner walls of hollow masonry units.

solid concrete like that of Figure B. The wall of concrete block is not only hollow but is traversed by joints (too frequently not solidly filled with mortar) which are the weak points in such an assembly. Basement walls of rough stone laid in Portland cement mortar should offer good resistance to lateral forces mainly because

CONSTRUCTION AND ARP

of their relatively great thickness (generally 16 to 24 inches). Much greater stability could be built into poured concrete walls with the introduction of a quantity of steel reinforcement. A typical form of failure due to earth shock is illustrated in Figure 15, C.

IV. SHELTERS

AIR-RAID SHELTERS of various shapes, sizes, materials, and methods of construction have been used abroad to good advantage. Authorities explain that the loss of life in England has not been large when one considers the tons of bombs that have been dumped on the island. This relatively small loss of life is explainable in part by the facts that the people were alert and that shelters had been prepared. Statistics show that "casualties in shelters constituted a very small percentage of all casualties, despite the fact that a rather large percentage of the people is estimated to have been sheltering at the time of the raids."[1]

Many perplexing and complicated questions arise in connection with the shelter problem because there is no universal solution. At the present time it would be irrational to attempt to provide perfect protection for all; in fact, it would be economically and physically impossible to do so. Such shelters as we can provide afford varying degrees of protection according to their geographical location, the stability of the materials, and the system of construction.

It should be recognized that buildings as they already exist do, in themselves, provide some protection. However, because of widely different economic and social

[1] "Air Raid Shelters," an address by John E. Burchard (Executive Officer, Committee on Passive Protection against Bombing, National Academy of Science), delivered at the National Conference on Air Raid Precautions, New York, 1942.

SHELTERS

conditions, a great many persons unfortunately live in extremely vulnerable buildings, while others live in less vulnerable structures, and a few others live in buildings relatively invulnerable. Persons living in urban areas in (1) "old law" tenements, (2) converted dwellings, (3) frame houses, (4) brick or row houses, (5) nonfireproof apartment houses, and (6) fireproof buildings are vulnerable to danger in about this order.

As to suburban and rural districts, the range of building types is not generally as great as in the city. Nevertheless, the degree of risk, in so far as building construction is concerned—but not geographical location—will vary in the same way as in the urban districts.

Air-raid protection is accomplished in a variety of ways. Some homes are so planned that refuge rooms may be provided without much effort; again, the construction of shelter areas may be the logical way to provide necessary protection in other instances; or, under still different conditions, outdoor shelters, either above or below ground, may prove to be desirable.

Shelters in Existing Buildings

Wood frame buildings:—The home of light wood frame construction covered with wood or composition materials, as ordinarily planned and constructed, does not provide much protection. As stated above, there are no data from actual bombings to judge its behavior by, because American frame construction is lighter and less rigidly assembled than its bomb-tested European proto-

SHELTERS

types. Similar construction in England has not fared well under bombardment. Government tests in this country also indicate that it is the least resistive of the

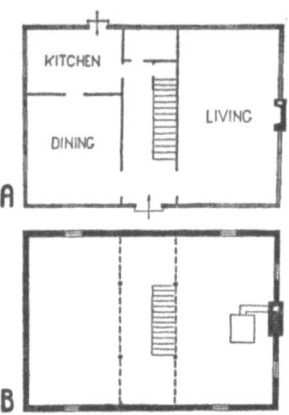

16. TYPICAL PLAN OF THE FRAME HOUSE

A, a first-floor plan which, with slight variations, is typical of many homes. The hollow wood framed walls of these houses afford the least amount of protection of any of the usual systems of construction. Likewise the floors and roofs of this construction offer little overhead protection. Probably the safest existing location is to be found in the first-floor hall. The basement (B), being less vulnerable to blast and fragmentation, provides a safer location if the basement ceiling is reinforced as shown in Fig. 21.

several types of construction.[2] Consequently, refuge rooms above grade in this class of building afford the least protection. Recalling facts previously brought out in the analysis of this construction and looking

[2]Office of Civilian Defense, *Report of Bomb Tests on Materials and Structures*, Washington, D. C., 1941. See also data in Appendix, concerning resistance of materials.

SHELTERS

at Figure 16, A, which shows a plan typical of thousands of American homes, it is difficult to find a location which will give much protection. Probably the first-floor hall will afford the best refuge, as this area is protected by two walls on three of its sides and by one wall on the fourth. All walls are pierced by openings which decrease protection. Overhead protection is not adequate in the event of the collapse of the upper portion of the house; in fact, it is possible that the floor underfoot would not support the debris from above in such an event. Such buildings are also especially vulnerable to fire. It would seem inadvisable, therefore, to expend any effort on money to increase the safety of such an area. Probably, as will be shown later, an area in the basement would afford greater protection.

Masonry veneer buildings:—Masonry veneer houses (brick, stone, or similar material) when subjected to bombardment behave identically in every way with other light wood frame structures with different exterior coverings, except that the masonry veneer does provide slightly more protection against blast, fragmentation, and splinters.

Wall-bearing buildings:—Many single-family solid brick wall-bearing houses are built with plans similar to that shown on Figure 16. Because of the inherently greater resistance of solid masonry to blast, fragmentation, and splinters, a refuge area in the hall, as suggested above, would provide more protection than would such an

SHELTERS

area in a wood frame house. However, protection overhead and support underfoot are no greater, because the roof and floor constructions are identical in both cases. The masonry house, because of the inelastic quality of masonry, is highly vulnerable to earth shock, and if collapse should occur the debris load of masonry would be dangerous. Of course the wood frame building rests upon masonry foundations which are just as vulnerable to earth shock as is the masonry house; but the frame superstructure is more elastic and would probably be less likely to disintegrate from earth shock than the wall-bearing structure.

Hazard of attic:—Almost invariably, when pitched or sloping roofs are installed on residence structures, attic spaces are created. The customary use of this space is such as to make it, together with the way it is constructed, a most hazardous place. That is to say, the amount of inflammable material generally stored in the attic and the fragility of the roof construction invite disaster through attack by incendiary bombs. The roof structure is not only the most vulnerable from the point of attack —the bombs are dropped from overhead—but it is the thinnest construction in the whole building. Figure 17 illustrates a typical attic space, except that the usual confusion and miscellaneous collection of things is not shown. It will be observed that there is very little material in the roof structure. If wood shingles form the roof covering, there is generally no continuous or solid layer of boarding underneath the shingles, shingle lath

SHELTERS

or sticks with open spaces between being used as shown. Even when composition roofing or slates are used and a solid boarding is placed under them, this boarding is less than one inch thick. The attic shown in the draw-

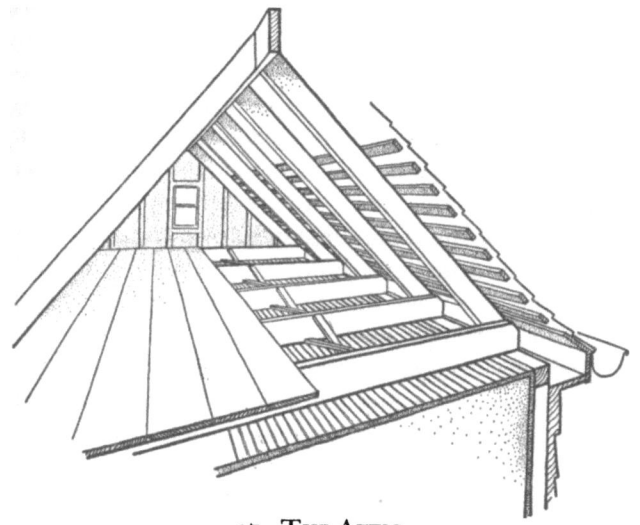

17. THE ATTIC

The fragility of its construction and the fact that bombs can easily penetrate it are apparent. Even an incendiary may penetrate the thin roofing and land on the inflammable attic flooring, or if the attic is not floored, the bomb may even penetrate the ceiling of the room below. Combustible objects, furniture, papers, etc., if stored in this space very greatly increase the fire hazard.

ing is not "finished," and consequently the only materials between the exterior and interior space are at best the roof boards and the roofing material, probably less than two inches in thickness over all. But even when

SHELTERS

a "finish" such as plaster, wallboard, or plywood is installed, relatively little more thickness and therefore little more resistance to bomb penetration is added. Experience abroad has shown that even the blunt-nosed kilo-incendiary bomb will often penetrate this type of roof construction. If one of these bombs penetrates the roof surface, its journey will probably be terminated on the attic floor—if the attic has a floor. The flooring in many attics does not extend from wall to wall. If such be the case, the only material to resist the travel of the bomb is the finish, usually lath and plaster, on the ceiling of the room directly below. The attic floor of such a construction is shown to the right in the drawing. If the attic is not floored over, the bomb may land on the floor below the attic level.

Many devices and materials have been suggested for use on or above the attic floor level to reduce the hazard of the incendiary. One suggested material which has found popular favor is sand: a layer of sand two or three inches deep is spread on the floor, which is protected by a layer of heavy building paper. This is undoubtedly a good stopper layer. Before using this method, one should make sure the floor can support this added weight, which may be a ton or more (dry loose sand weighs 90 to 100 pounds a cubic foot). Dry sifted earth and ashes also have been suggested. It would seem that the dust from these materials, which will be blown about by the air currents usually present in the attic, constitutes an objection to their use. Furthermore, the use of such materials as these precludes the use of the

SHELTERS

attic for any other purpose whatsoever. On the other hand, sand, ashes, and earth are inexpensive and easily placed. A number of synthetic board materials on the market that are light in weight, reasonably strong, and fireproof probably would if installed in adequate thickness, form better stopper layers. Fireproof protection of exposed parts of the construction adjacent to the floor to a height of about four feet has been recommended, and in low, small spaces where vigorous action in fighting a fire bomb is difficult, such protection is desirable. Several fire-resisting paints made of artificial resins are available and may be used for this purpose.

Row houses:—In some instances the walls enclosing stair halls in row houses of wall-bearing construction are also built of masonry. Many row houses in the metropolitan areas are erected with plans similar to that shown on Figure 18. In such cases the halls afford refuge areas safer from blast and fragmentation than space in any of the types cited above. Perhaps the next best location is the kitchen, whose only exposed wall is small. All other sides of the kitchen are provided considerable protection by fire walls and partitions. Considerably more safety could be given this room by erecting a masonry screen wall, as shown at Figure C. However, from above and below, these houses are as vulnerable as the wood frame constructions. They are also as vulnerable to earth shock as other wall-bearing buildings.

SHELTERS

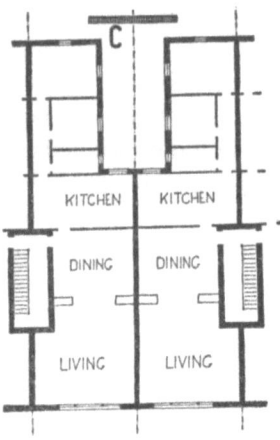

18. ROW-HOUSE PLAN

These buildings with roofs and floors of wood construction are vulnerable from above and, being of wall-bearing construction, they are also vulnerable to earth shock. Considerable lateral protection is provided however by their masonry walls, and in this respect the greatest amount of protection will be found in the stair hall. The next best shelter will be found in the kitchen, especially if a masonry screen is provided, to minimize blast and fragmentation effects, as shown at C.

Tenement houses and converted dwellings:—A study of the plans of a tenement house shown on Figure 19, A, and a converted dwelling, Figure 19, B, both of which are of wall-bearing construction, will convince one that no reasonably safe refuge area can be found in these buildings. The majority of such structures do not have a single piece of masonry or other stable fireproof construction in their interior. It is of course true that these buildings provide in their hallways and similar interior

SHELTERS

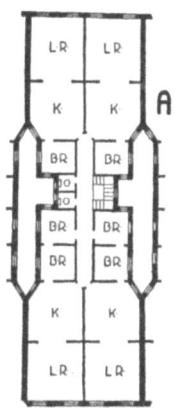 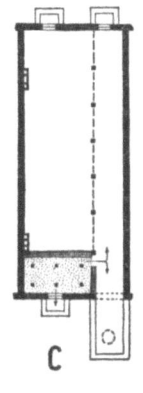 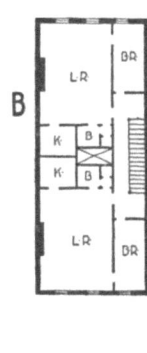

19. Tenement and Converted Building Plans

Thousands of all tenement buildings (similar to A), are extant with interior parts made of wood. Like other non-fireproof wall-bearing buildings, these houses offer little protection. As in the case of other attached dwellings some lateral protection is afforded by their exterior masonry walls, but overhead protection is negligible. If conditions should seem to justify providing shelter within any of these structures, a reinforced area in the basement would probably prove to be the best solution. Many buildings, formerly single-family city houses, have been so altered as now to contain several apartments or in other cases have become rooming houses. These buildings fall in about the same category as the tenement. The facts that the population of these buildings is smaller and that the buildings are usually but three or four stories high reduce somewhat the hazard. B is a reasonably typical plan of a converted building. C, a general basement plan which is similar to basements of both tenement and converted buildings. The shaded area is suggested as a possible location for a reinforced basement shelter. Use is made of two of the foundation walls (usually built of rubblestone masonry 2 feet or more in thickness) to form two sides of the shelter. The other two sides may be formed with sandbags or masonry. The reinforcing of the ceiling is built as shown on Fig. 21. Every basement shelter should have at least two exits.

spaces as much protection as does the wall-bearing dwelling already discussed. But it must be remembered that in the case of the single dwelling the average height of such houses is not over two or at the most three stories and that their population is small, whereas the tenement may be six stories high and house many families. The converted dwelling, often four or five stories in height, also houses many persons. It would seem, therefore, that tenements and converted dwellings as they exist today constitute a hazard, by virtue of their construction, to great numbers of people and that the designating of refuge areas in these buildings is unwise. In the past few years many of these buildings in New York City have had the stairs and stair halls "fire-retarded"—made fire resistant—and less hazardous fire escapes have been installed. These features, while of value under ordinary conditions, do not increase their safety to any appreciable extent in so far as air-raid protection is concerned, except in respect to fire when the building remains standing.

Modern nonfireproof apartment houses:—Figure 20 shows a typical plan and a "phantom" elevational illustration of a modern ("new law") nonfireproof six-story apartment house or multiple dwelling. These buildings, although of wall-bearing construction, differ from the tenement houses in that the stairs and stair halls from street to roof are built with walls and floors of fireproof construction. These means of egress form a fireproof core in the interior of these buildings. A

SHELTERS

greater degree of safety is provided in a refuge area on the second or third floor in the hall of one of these buildings than in any of the buildings discussed above. That such a refuge area as this does not give complete protection, however, is evident because the floor construction adjacent to the halls is wood frame and is as vulnerable as it is in any of the other nonfireproof buildings. But the area is provided with considerable protection from blast and fragmentation, originating on the outside, by two masonry walls. The fireproof floors in the halls, which are constructed like the floor shown on Figure 12, do afford much more overhead

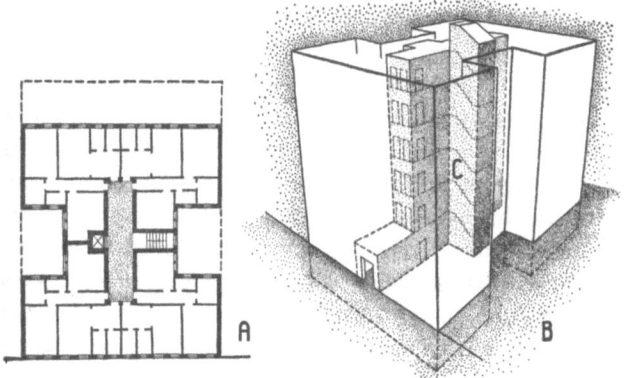

20. MODERN NON-FIREPROOF APARTMENT HOUSES

A, a plan common to many of these buildings. The second and third floor public halls, the shaded area on the plan, having substantial fireproof floors (similar to that shown on Fig. 12) and masonry enclosing walls, affords the best shelter areas in these buildings. This fireproof "core" containing the public halls, extends vertically through the building from street to roof.

SHELTERS

protection and adequate protection from incendiaries. Perhaps the weakest point about this assembly is its wall-bearing construction and consequent vulnerability to earth shock.

Fireproof skeleton construction:—The term "fireproof multiple dwelling" generally includes both apartment houses and hotel buildings. These buildings have a skeleton either of steel or of reinforced concrete (generally steel) that is exceedingly stable. Refuge areas in these buildings are the safest to be found in any normal structure anywhere. Such areas, to provide the highest degree of safety, should be located in interior spaces and on the intermediate floors. A shelter located, say, five, six, or more floors below the roof will have overhead protection sufficient to stop many of the heavier bombs, and if the shelter is four or more stories above the street the blast and fragment hazard from bombs exploding on the ground will be largely eliminated. Because throughout the entire height of these buildings the walls are relatively thin and also because the wide expanse of these walls offers a large target for bombs falling at an angle (as all bombs do), it is necessary to locate shelter areas as far away from the perimeter of the building as possible. Incendiary bombs are not a hazard to these buildings. Earth shock will have less effect on this construction than on any other type. The foundations are not continuous masonry walls but isolated pieces of masonry which support the vertical posts or columns. The isolated foundations do not transmit

SHELTERS

earth shock to other foundations as readily as would a continuous foundation. Furthermore, this construction is much more elastic than is the masonry construction.

Basement Shelters

The foregoing discussion would indicate that no area in the superstructure of the frame house, masonry veneer house, wall-bearing house, row house, tenement, or converted dwelling is comfortably safe, although some areas in some of these buildings are safer than others. However, another space in these structures under certain conditions will provide reasonably safe shelter: the basement. The basement has both advantages and disadvantages, and authorities are by no means in agreement on the advisability of using the basement as a shelter area.

The basement, being below grade level, is protected by the earth from the effects of blast and fragmentation. The floor of any basement shelter area is safe, being supported by the earth below. The most vulnerable part of this space is the ceiling, which, since the upper part of the structure may collapse, should be strengthened. Figure 21 illustrates a method of reinforcing the floor immediately above the basement. The reinforcement is essentially a stout platform built directly beneath this floor, which forms the ceiling of the basement. The horizontal beams A, which support the heavy platform flooring B, are in turn entirely supported by the posts C. These beams should not be sup-

SHELTERS

ported at any point by the foundation walls; in fact they should not extend within several inches of the walls. If the beams are thus installed, failure of the wall—perhaps because of earth shock—will not necessarily endanger the reinforcing or platform. The columns or posts should be securely fastened with wedges to the horizontal beams on the floor and at the ceiling; these floor beams distribute the weight of the platform. The wedges, which in turn should be made fast, are to prevent dislodgment of the posts, which might otherwise occur as a result of lateral earth movement through earth shock. As most basement floors are larger

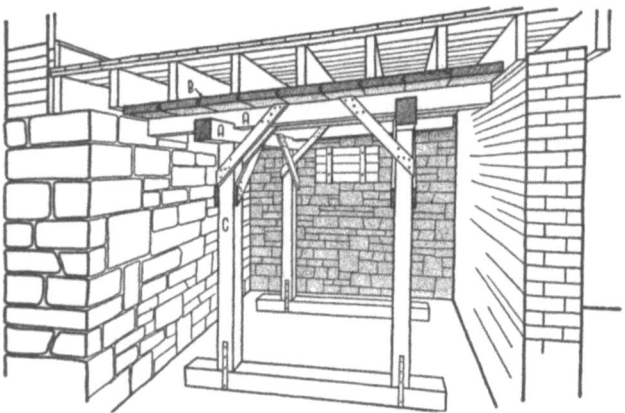

21. BASEMENT REINFORCING

A method of reinforcing the floor immediately above the basement, which forms the ceiling of the shelter. This method has been used to good advantage abroad. It consists essentially of a stout platform built underneath and against the basement ceiling. This platform and all supporting parts should be kept clear of the adjoining walls.

SHELTERS

than the shelter need be, a substantial masonry or sandbag wall may be built to inclose the shelter area.

The matter of egress from a basement shelter must be given thorough consideration. The location increases the hazard of being entrapped in the event of the collapse of the building overhead. Consequently, two well-planned and well-located exits should be a minimum requirement for every shelter.

It goes without saying that shovels, picks, sand, water, and similar materials and implements should be standard equipment for every shelter.

The location of sewer, water and gas pipes, and electrical lines, as well as heating equipment, whether coal or oil, must be considered when the exact location of the shelter area in the basement is being determined. It is obvious that these services, in so far as possible, should be outside the shelter area and that controls for shutting off such of these services as can be so controlled be in good order.

Morrison Shelter

The discomforts experienced in the Anderson outdoor shelter (described below) undoubtedly prompted the development of the so-called table shelter or Morrison shelter, which, incidentally, is a very poor table. This shelter is merely a stout rectangular box large enough to accommodate a wide mattress. The vertical sides of this box are covered with heavy wire netting, which will not protect from fragments; the top is of sheet metal. The framework, made of metal shapes,

SHELTERS

supports the metal top, and the frame and top are made strong enough to hold the debris load of the building in which the shelter is located so that anyone within the shelter will not be harmed. It is obvious that this shelter must be located behind walls which will stop splinters and on a floor which either is not over a basement or a cellar unless the floor is reinforced suf-

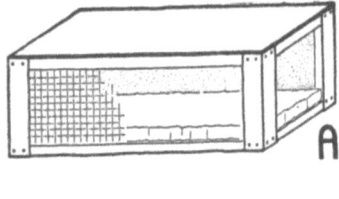

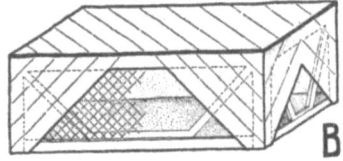

22. THE MORRISON SHELTER

The frame (A), built of metal shapes bolted together, is covered by heavy sheet metal on top and by heavy wire screening on the sides. Measuring about 4 feet by 7 feet, accommodates a wide mattress. When this shelter is used, protection against blast and fragmentation is assumed to be provided by the walls of the building in which it is placed. B, a similar shelter made of wood. A substantial top, made with one-inch boards securely fastened to both the top and bottom sides of 2 inch by 4 inch beams, is supported by heavily braced uprights. A stout floor is also provided. Means of egress, from all four sides, is through openings in the diagonal boarding forming the sides. These openings are protected by heavy wire screening. This shelter is used in the same way and under the same conditions as the Morrison Shelter. More complete data on this shelter will be found in the *Architectural Forum*, Jan., 1942.

SHELTERS

ficiently to carry the debris load of the building. These table shelters may be in the basement, but this adds the problem of escape, which should make us approach their use and placing with considerable caution. Nevertheless, they do have a value when rightly used 22, A shows one of these shelters.

Outdoor Shelters

Individual outdoor shelters will undoubtedly be considered as a likely solution for the shelter problem by many persons living in suburban areas where there is ample space adjacent to the house. Available space is not, however, the governing factor in determining whether or not to locate the shelter outdoors. Many buildings are so planned that it is not only inconvenient but also impractical to make use of any part of them for shelter purposes. Others may be of poor construction or especially vulnerable to fire or near an important target; such buildings are worse than no shelter. Furthermore, the expense involved will in most instances be a major factor and can not be overlooked.

Outdoor shelters are frequently classified by their position with respect to the surface of the ground: surface, semisurface, and subsurface. *Surface shelters* are vulnerable to blast and fragments but not to earth shock, to any very great degree. *Semisurface shelters* are somewhat less endangered by blast and fragments but more by earth shock. The *subsurface* or *buried shelter* is immune to blast and fragments but most vulnerable to

SHELTERS

earth shock. A shelter deep in the earth provides complete safety. However, the depth required for complete protection — some 60 or 70 feet in certain soils — is so great as to render such a shelter impracticable.

In addition to the effects of the attack on the shelter, conditions imposed by the character of the soil, by the location of public utilities, and by personal comfort must be carefully considered before a wise decision can be made as to the type and location of an outdoor shelter. The location of sewer and water, gas, and electric supplies must be reckoned with not only because these services must not be disturbed if normal living habits are to continue but also because their rupture may be a hazard to occupants of the buried or half-buried shelter. The nature of the topography and the level of groundwater must also be considered. Another factor, that of temperature, must not be overlooked. It has been found in England that outdoor shelters become uncomfortable if occupied for any considerable length of time. Many raids have been of longer duration than was expected, and as a result there has been a tendency to abandon many of the small subsurface shelters. The amenities of such a shelter are few, and when one must be occupied throughout the greater part of the night, mere discomfort may become actual endangering of health.

Anderson shelter: — A semisurface shelter extensively used in England should be examined: the shelter devised by Sir John Anderson, shown on Figure 23. It is

SHELTERS

made usually of thin sheet steel or corrugated iron. It is designed to be partially buried and to be covered by about two feet of earth, which minimizes the chance of its being pierced by fragments. In effect, this shelter forms a support for an arch of earth. It has proved of

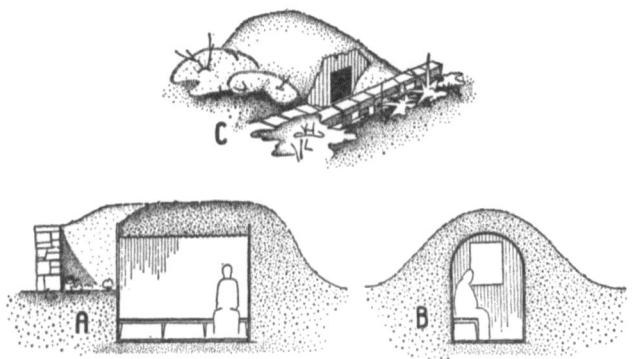

23. THE ANDERSON SHELTER

This shelter, made of corrugated sheet metal, is designed to be installed so that its floor (of tamped earth, stone paving, or planking) is three or four feet below grade. The earth, together with the earth cover placed over the shelter, provides protection from blast and fragmentation. A screen wall (of stone or other material) provides protection for the entrance (A), which is a longitudinal section thru the shelter. A cross-section is shown at B, and a general view at C.

value for several reasons: it is small and consequently its chance of being hit is reduced; it is generally installed in the yard where the earth is soft so that bombs tend to penetrate the surface before exploding and thus to spend part of their destructive energy harmlessly and to reduce fragmentation; and it is somewhat elastic and

SHELTERS

therefore tends to yield to earth shock rather than to fracture. These shelters are not invulnerable to very near hits even of small bombs. They will in general withstand a hit far enough away so that the shelter is outside of the crater radius, which might be, under certain conditions, approximately 8 feet for a 100-pound bomb and 20 feet, more or less, for a 500-pound bomb.

Full-scale explosion tests, made with 500-pound medium-case bombs detonated on the surface of the ground and at a depth of 4 feet below the surface, with the shelters placed 1 foot and 3 feet below the ground, have shown that these shelters provide adequate protection under these conditions; no damage to the shelters resulted, though there was some disturbance of the earth cover on the side nearest the explosions. In fact, tests have shown that except for the disturbance of the earth cover, these shelters were not injured by blast from explosions of the 500-pound bombs even as close as 25 feet.[3]

Metal tubular shelter: — Corrugated metal, such as is used for the Anderson shelter is the material also of a fundamentally different form of shelter. Figure 24, A, a sectional diagram, shows this cylindrical corrugated heavy metal tube shelter, 6 feet 3 inches in diameter, installed with an earth cover of at least 1½ or 2 feet. The entrance to the shelter from the basement of the

[3] For more complete data concerning these and physiological tests, see *Sectional Steel Shelters*, His Majesty's Stationery Office, London, 1939.

SHELTERS

house is through a smaller metal tube (3 feet in diameter), and a second entrance or exit, at the opposite end, is provided by a similar tube, the far end of which is protected at the surface by a masonry or sandbag barricade. Figure B, a cross-sectional view of the interior,

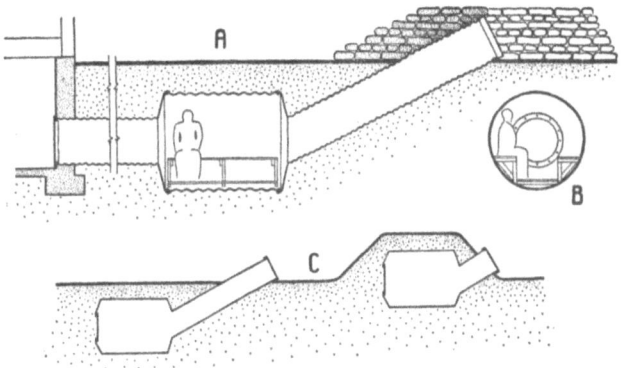

24. METAL TUBULAR SHELTER

An American version of the metal shelter is shown on this drawing. It is essentially a large (6 feet by 3 inches in diameter) corrugated sheet-metal pipe. Despite the fact that sub-surface shelters are especially vulnerable, to earth shock, during tests this shelter behaved exceptionally well. Its flexible quality is an asset. A longitudinal section A, suggests a method of installing with entrance from the basement of the house. Section B, is a cross section. Other methods of installing are shown at C.

shows the circular form of the shelter. Figure C illustrates its installation as a subsurface and as a semisurface shelter. Tests proved this shelter, because of its tube form and elastic quality, to be very resistant to earth-shock waves from all directions except against its ends.

SHELTERS

(This fact suggests that a sphere would be the ideal form.) Like the Anderson shelter, the metal tube shelter depends on its earth cover to dissipate blast and fragmentation effects.

The metal tube shelter was tested by statically detonating two 300-pound and five 600-pound bombs at distances of 10 to 30 feet from the shelter. Even though the shelter was within the crater area of one of the 600-pound bombs, it was not demolished. The 600-pound bombs exploded at distances of 10 and 15 feet away raised an end of the shelter from $2\frac{1}{2}$ to $3\frac{1}{2}$ feet and moved it laterally about $1\frac{1}{2}$ feet. The explosions also "dished in" a part of the shelter as much as $1\frac{1}{2}$ feet on the lower side. A considerable amount of the earth cover was also removed from the top and side of the shelter.

Reinforced concrete shelters: — Masonry materials are also used in constructing shelters. A broad plain and reinforced brickwork has been used as well as reinforced concrete, which seems to be especially suitable for these purposes. Obviously, masonry materials are most satisfactory from the point of view of durability. Subsurface shelters of reinforced concrete approximately 5 by 6 feet inside and 6 feet 6 inches high, built with walls, floors, and roofs 8 inches thick and covered with earth about 3 feet deep have been tested by statically detonated bombs. Though the shelter tested was damaged (the wall near the explosion was cracked) as a result of the explosion of a 300-pound bomb 10 feet away and a 600-pound bomb 30 feet away, the shelter did not col-

SHELTERS

lapse.[4] However, the behavior of this and other similar shelters has indicated the necessity of additional reinforcement at the junctions of the walls, floors, and roof as well as the necessity for increasing the floor thickness of subsurface shelters to resist the effect of earth shock.

A general view of a reinforced concrete shelter is shown on Figure 25, A. It consists of a single room with a vestibule or screen wall to protect the door shown in one end of the shelter. A second opening to serve as an emergency exit is provided in the opposite end. A cross-sectional view is illustrated at B, where the recommended additional reinforcing is indicated at the four corners.

It has been recommended that the roof slabs of these shelters be made 6 inches thick, the walls 12 inches thick, and the floor 9 inches thick, as tests already made on other shelters indicate that these thicknesses will provide relatively substantial protection.[5]

As this type of shelter is of a durable nature, it would seem to be advantageous to fix its location with respect to the general arrangement of the yard or garden so that a double use could be made of it, if local conditions permit. Figure 25, C, illustrates this idea. During the emergency it functions as a shelter; later it would serve well

[4]Complete data on this and other tests will be found in *Report of Bomb Tests on Materials and Structures: Memorandum on Protective Construction,* issued by the U. S. Office of Civilian Defense, Washington, D. C., 1941.

[5]From the address of John E. Burchard, Executive Officer, Committee on Passive Protection against Bombing, National Academy of Science, before the National Conference at New York City, 1942.

SHELTERS

as a tool shed or a root cellar. While it functions as a shelter, the entrance door, which as shown is not protected by a vestibule, should be screened by a barricade built on the retaining wall shown in front of the entrance.

The vulnerability of subsurface shelters to earth shock and surface shelters to blast and fragmentation has

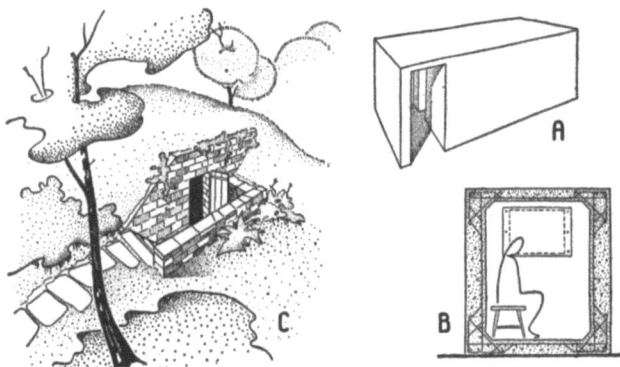

25. A REINFORCED CONCRETE SHELTER

A, a boxlike shelter of reinforced concrete; a vestibule or wall protecting the entrance is shown as an integral part of the shelter. B, a cross section of the shelter showing the diagonal reinforcing at the corners. C, a general view of the shelter is a semi-surface location. It should be remembered that a baffle wall, to protect the entrance, is highly important.

raised the question as to which position is the better for an outdoor shelter. In other words, which of these destructive forces can be most successfully combatted so that a maximum of protection is afforded by the shelter. At the present time, available data do not show con-

[74]

SHELTERS

clusively the complete superiority of one location over the other when all factors involved are considered. However, some authorities believe that tests tend to indicate that "the hazards of the semiburied shelter or the shelter just below the surface of the earth are such that they should not be used whenever a surface shelter is possible."[6] Reports to be issued by the Office of Civilian Defense will give additional information on this question.

[6]*Ibid.*

V. MATERIALS AND CONSTRUCTION

Tests of Materials

A GENERAL evaluation of the materials and methods of construction which may be utilized in providing air-raid shelter is difficult because the reactions of structures under bombing are very different from their reactions under usual conditions and because site, soil, methods of construction, size and type of bomb, proximity of explosion to shelter, and other factors must all be considered.

Results of actual tests on certain materials and constructions furnish data for specific conditions of exposure and are therefore of value. A digest of the results of some of these tests follows. In the first test, panels of various materials 5 feet high and 10 feet wide were buttressed with sandbags and arranged at equal intervals along the circumference of a circle with a radius of 50 feet. A 600-pound demolition bomb was detonated in the center of the circle, with the following results:

1. A wood frame stud wall with wood sheathing and wood siding received 15 perforations and 4 penetrations of $1\frac{1}{8}$ inches maximum depth. The panel remained standing.

2. A brick wall 12 inches thick, provided with a concrete frame for support, received no perforations and 20 penetrations of 2 inches maximum depth. The panel was damaged very little.

MATERIALS AND CONSTRUCTION

3. A sandbag wall 30 inches thick, received no perforations and 31 penetrations of $5\frac{1}{2}$ inches maximum depth. Two courses of sandbags at an end were blown over.

4. A structural steel plate $\frac{1}{2}$ inch thick, supported by a wood frame, received 2 perforations and 27 penetrations of 9-16 of an inch maximum depth. The panel was not otherwise damaged.

5. A hollow cinder block wall 8 inches thick, surrounded by a frame of 12-by-12-inch timbers, received 2 perforations and 13 penetrations of $1\frac{1}{2}$ inches maximum depth. The panel was not otherwise damaged.

6. A standard brick veneer wall with wood sheathing, with 4 inches of brick on the outside, and with wire lath and plaster on the inside received 2 perforations and 23 penetrations of $1\frac{3}{4}$ inches maximum depth. This wall was cracked in several places.

7. Two equal sections of a panel of 10-gauge and 12-gauge corrugated iron attached to a wood frame received respectively 12 and 18 perforations and 8 and 5 penetrations of $\frac{1}{4}$ inch maximum depth. The panel was moved slightly by blast and the sheets were warped slightly, but there was no other damage.

8. A panel was built in two equal sections, one section having one layer of $\frac{3}{4}$-inch plywood fastened to the front side of 2-by-4-inch wood studs and one layer of $\frac{3}{4}$-inch plywood fastened to the rear side of the studs, the other section having 2 layers of $\frac{3}{4}$-inch plywood fastened to one side of the studs. The two sec-

MATERIALS AND CONSTRUCTION

tions of this panel received respectively 9 and 8 perforations and 5 and 3 penetrations of $\frac{3}{4}$ and 1 inch maximum depth. The panel remained in place.

In the second test the same panels were arranged equidistant from each other along the circumference of a circle with a radius of 25 feet. A 300-pound bomb was detonated in the center of the circle, with the following results:

1. was blown to bits and scattered about.

2. had a large hole in the top and 15 penetrations of 6 inches maximum depth. Previous penetration were enlarged.

3. received 15 penetrations of $7\frac{1}{2}$ inches maximum depth. The bags were blown over, except those of the six bottom courses.

4. received 11 perforations and 102 penetrations of $\frac{7}{8}$ of an inch maximum depth. The panel was blown over.

5. received 5 perforations and 39 penetrations of $2\frac{1}{4}$ inches maximum depth. The wall was blown over, except for the two bottom courses.

6. received 10 penetrations of $1\frac{3}{4}$ inches maximum depth. The upper portion of the panel was shattered.

7. showed these effect: the 10-gauge and 12-gauge sections received respectively 8 and 40 perforations and 60 and 57 penetrations of 3/16 of an inch maximum

MATERIALS AND CONSTRUCTION

depth. The panel was blown over. No other change was noted.[1]

Classifications of Structures

The Department of Housing and Building of New York city has classified, in terms of construction and the protection afforded by the construction, all buildings in the city. As the various types of construction are common to all communities, the list is of interest to everyone. Furthermore, the Department has made recommendations regarding the locations in each type of building which in general afford the safest shelter. The classifications are as follows:

1. Fireproof buildings over 10 stories in height with steel or concrete fireproof frames
2. Fireproof buildings less than 10 stories in height with steel or concrete fireproof frames
3. Fireproof buildings, wall-bearing type
4. Nonfireproof buildings, wall-bearing type, with interior areas of refuge.
5. Nonfireproof buildings, wall-bearing type, without interior areas of refuge
6. Converted dwellings (wall-bearing; nonfireproof; for the most part 5 stories or less in height)

[1] These data are from *Report of Bomb Tests on Materials and Structures: Memorandum on Protective Construction*, published by the United States Office of Civilian Defense, in which pamphlet more complete data on these and other tests will be found.

MATERIALS AND CONSTRUCTION

7. Frame buildings
8. Low buildings with large floor areas, such as one- and two-story taxpayers, railroad stations, bus terminals, theaters, churches, skating rinks, and dance halls

The Department recommended the following locations as, in general, the safest portions of the buildings during air raids:

Class 1: Occupants should remain above the second story and at least 5 stories down from the roof.

Class 2: Remain above the second story and down at least 3 stories from the roof.
NOTE: In both the above cases a setback roof should be considered the same as the main roof of the building.

Class 3: In this type of building, except where there are interior bays, the safest location is in the basement provided it has two relatively remote means of egress. (The word *bay* is used here to denote the space between interior supporting columns or supporting exterior walls or columns and interior columns.) In buildings with interior bays, use such spaces above the second floor and down at least 3 stories from the roof. In residence buildings, use basements, keep away from yard windows, and wherever possible use a portion of the basement alongside a wall which is retaining the earth on the outside. If there is within the basement an interior

MATERIALS AND CONSTRUCTION

area surrounded by masonry walls, this area would be the most acceptable in the basement.

Class 4: Use the basement of this type of building, as in Class 3; and, in addition, if there are any areas above the first floor and below the top floor which are enclosed in masonry walls, these areas may also be used.

Classes 5 and 6: Use the basements in these two classes of buildings, provided the basements are so arranged that there are at least two means of egress from them and that there are no unusual hazards such as live steam mains or gas mains which cannot be shut off outside the basements. However, it is advisable that certain reinforcement be added to the basement for the support of the first tier of beams. If there is no such basement for a building, the best area is an interior room as near the center of the building as possible, or a room alongside a party masonry wall above the first floor and below the top floor.

Class 7: In frame buildings, particularly the one- and two-story residential buildings, the basement is the safest portion. However, it is advisable that certain reinforcement be added to the basement for the support of the first tier of beams. Also, additional means of egress should be provided from the basement unless two already exist.

Class 8: Complete evacuation is recommended for occupants of this class of building.

BIBLIOGRAPHY

IN ADDITION to the books listed below, many handbooks and pamphlets published by the British Government are available at the British Library of Information, R.C.A. Building, New York, New York.

The United States Information Service maintains an office at 521 Fifth Avenue, New York, New York, where many defense pamphlets may be obtained.

Architectural Forum, civil defense reference number, Vol. LXXVI, No. 1 (January, 1942).

Great Britain, Ministry of Home Security. Directions for the Erection of Domestic Surface Shelters. London, H.M. Stationery Office, 1939.

Great Britain, Office of the Lord Privy Seal. Sectional Steel Shelters. London, H.M. Stationery Office, 1939.

Ley, Willy. Bombs and Bombing. New York, Modern Age, 1941.

Prentiss, Augustin M. Civil Air Defense. New York, McGraw-Hill, 1941.

Snyder, Louis L., editor. Handbook of Civilian Protection, prepared by the Civilian Defense Council of the College of the City of New York. New York, McGraw-Hill, 1942.

Tecton (firm, architects). Planned A.R.P. Westminster, Architectural Press, 1939; Brooklyn, N. Y., Chemical Publishing Co., 1941.

BIBLIOGRAPHY

United States Office of Civilian Defense. Protective Construction. Structure Series, No. 1. Washington, D. C., United States Government Printing Office, 1941.

––– Standard School Lectures: Civilian Protection. Series II, Fire Defense, sections D and E. Washington, D. C., United States Government Printing Office, 1942.

United States War Department. Report of Bomb Tests on Materials and Structures. Memorandum on Protective Construction. Washington, D. C., United States Office of Civilian Defense, 1941.

Wessman, Harold E., and William A. Rose. Aerial Bombardment Protection. New York, John Wiley, 1942.

Zanetti, J. Enrique. Fire from the Air. New York, Columbia University Press, 1942.

COLUMBIA HOME FRONT WARBOOKS

Facts and Ideas for Americans Working for Victory

1. **FIRE FROM THE AIR; the A B C of Incendiaries**
   By J. Enrique Zanetti, Professor of Chemistry, Columbia University. 64 pages. Illustrated. 50 cents.
   Time says of the author: "the No. 1 U. S. pyrotechnician"; of the pamphlet: "a concise handbook of arson."

2. **THIS INEVITABLE CONFLICT**
   By Carlton J. H. Hayes, United States Ambassador to Spain. 32 pages. 25 cents.
   The present war in historical perspective. Is it just another imperialistic and economic struggle?

3. **RELENTLESS WAR: the Key to Victory**
   By Edward Mead Earle, Institute for Advanced Study, Princeton, N. J. 32 pages. 25 cents.
   Present and past wars of the United States. The common cause and grand strategy.

4. **RESOURCES FOR VICTORY**
   By John E. Orchard, Professor of Economic Geography, Columbia University. 36 pages. 25 cents.
   Our natural resources. Their strategic use. What civilians must do without if we are to out-produce the Axis.

5. **FINANCING TOTAL WAR**
   By Robert Murray Haig, McVickar Professor of Political Economy, Columbia University. 32 pages. 25 cents.
   Objectives sought, and analysis and appraisal of methods for achieving them.

6. **PSYCHOLOGY: the Third Dimension of War**
   By Carroll C. Pratt, Professor of Psychology, Rutgers University. 29 pages. 25 cents.
   The meaning of psychological warfare. Its use by our enemies. How we can use this new weapon.

7. **BOMBS, BUILDINGS, AND SHELTERS; ARP for the Home**
   By William H. Hayes, Assistant Professor of Architecture, Columbia University. 84 pages. Illustrated. 60 cents.
   Explains the methods by which you can evaluate and provide air raid protection for your home and the people in it. Will save you time and money.

COLUMBIA UNIVERSITY PRESS
Morningside Heights, New York

Bei Fragen zur Produktsicherheit wenden Sie sich bitte an:
If you have any questions regarding product safety,
please contact:

Walter de Gruyter GmbH
Genthiner Straße 13
10785 Berlin
productsafety@degruyterbrill.com